Cambridge Elements ≡

Elements in Music since 1945
edited by
Mervyn Cooke
University of Nottingham

BAROQUE MUSIC IN POST-WAR CINEMA

Performance Practice and Musical Style

Donald Greig
University of Nottingham

CAMBRIDGE
UNIVERSITY PRESS

CAMBRIDGE
UNIVERSITY PRESS

University Printing House, Cambridge CB2 8BS, United Kingdom

One Liberty Plaza, 20th Floor, New York, NY 10006, USA

477 Williamstown Road, Port Melbourne, VIC 3207, Australia

314–321, 3rd Floor, Plot 3, Splendor Forum, Jasola District Centre,
New Delhi – 110025, India

79 Anson Road, #06–04/06, Singapore 079906

Cambridge University Press is part of the University of Cambridge.

It furthers the University's mission by disseminating knowledge in the pursuit of
education, learning, and research at the highest international levels of excellence.

www.cambridge.org
Information on this title: www.cambridge.org/9781108827867
DOI: 10.1017/9781108900614

First published 2021

A catalogue record for this publication is available from the British Library.

ISBN 978-1-108-82786-7 Paperback
ISSN 2632-7791 (online)
ISSN 2632-7783 (print)

Baroque Music in Post-War Cinema

Performance Practice and Musical Style

Elements in Music since 1945

DOI: 10.1017/9781108900614
First published online: February 2021

Donald Greig
University of Nottingham
Author for correspondence: Donald Greig, dongreig@gmail.com

Abstract: Studies of pre-existing music in narrative cinema often focus on a single film, composer or director. The approach here adopts a wider perspective, placing a specific musical repertoire – baroque music – in the context of its reception to explore its mobilisation in post-war cinema. It shows how various revivals have shaped musical fashion, and how cinema has drawn on resultant popularity and in turn contributed to it. Close analyses of various films raise issues of baroque musical style and form to question why eighteenth-century music remains an exception to dominant film-music discourses. Account is taken of changing modern performance practice and its manifestation in cinema, particularly in the biopic. This question of the re-imagining of baroque repertoire leads to consideration of pastiches and parodies to which cinema has been particularly drawn, and subsequently to the role that neo-baroque music has played in more recent films.

Keywords: baroque music, film music, neo-baroque music, historical performance practice, musical revivals

ISBNs: 9781108827867 (PB), 9781108900614 (OC)
ISSNs: 2632-7791 (online), 2632-7783 (print)

Contents

Introduction

It is a truism that more people will encounter classical music through popular media such as film and television than in the concert hall or from recordings. Yet despite this acknowledgement of a consumer with only a partial awareness or who is ignorant of musical history, studies of the use of classical music in cinema have often implied an idealised spectator with a privileged knowledge of the arcane history of repertoire and of musical styles. Such a strategy is familiar in other disciplines, of course, which have abandoned any search for individual response, celebrating instead textual and intertextual richness; the text is what it is, and potential readings are there to be divined. However, what is sometimes overlooked is the historical moment that informs the use of specific repertoire.

What follows is an essentially diachronic study of the use of baroque instrumental music in post-war films up to the present day. Films here provides a useful historiographical perspective on baroque repertoire in the twentieth and twenty-first centuries, demonstrating how musical style and currents of musical thinking have informed and to an extent determined cinematic practices. A short section on the use of baroque music in silent cinema establishes an important pre-war context and reveals many of the abiding connotations of baroque music in films – as a signifier of a generalised past, of religion, and of courtliness. Following this, I trace the history of the Vivaldi revival, the impact of which would be felt in cinema from the 1950s onwards. That revival, surely the most important baroque revival of the twentieth century, led to a new interest in, and a wholesale reassessment of, Italian baroque repertoire. This was soon manifest in films such as *Les Enfants terribles* (Jean-Pierre Melville, 1950) and *The Golden Coach* (Jean Renoir, 1952) which, in many respects, exemplify the main ways that baroque repertoire has been exploited up to the current day. *The Golden Coach, Dangerous Liaisons* (Stephen Frears, 1988) and *The Favourite* (Yorgos Lanthimos, 2018), for example, all begin with scenes where the protagonists are seen dressing for the day (a cinematic trope in period dramas, marking a separation between the private and public) to the accompaniment of music by Vivaldi or Handel. Premised on the coevality of the events depicted and the music heard, this essentially integrationist approach contrasts with a dissociative appropriation of similar repertoire. With their contemporary settings, *Pickpocket* (Robert Bresson, 1959), *Accattone* (Pier Paolo Pasolini, 1961) and *Mamma Roma* (Pier Paolo Pasolini, 1962) have no apparent connection to the music of eighteenth-century composers such as Fischer, Bach or Vivaldi. In Bresson's case, baroque music functions as punctuation while Pasolini's films provoke a sense of social and cultural dissociation. Lars von

Trier's use of baroque repertoire in *Dogville* (2003) and *Manderlay* (2005) revisits both approaches. Such variant practices rely in no small part on the music's readily identifiable stylistic features, particularly its repeated rhythmic patterns and its regular metres. While the fluid rhythms of the late-romantic music characteristic of the Hollywood studio era were always ultimately subordinate to the drama, shadowing and supporting it, the more rigid metrical designs and rhythmic formulae of baroque music suggest self-involved indifference, resistant to nuanced integration.

Accounts of these two general approaches to baroque music, the integrationist and the dissociative, are complemented by two shorter sections that explore different modalities of more modern re-imaginings of baroque repertoire, one performative, the other compositional. The first of these two final sections considers the role that performance practice has played in cinema, specifically that of historically informed performance (HIP). The way that Vivaldi was performed in *Les Enfants terribles* is considerably different from the music heard in *Manderlay* some fifty-five years later, and the range of potential meanings that film-makers could exploit has inevitably altered. HIP was a response to debates about authenticity conducted in the 1970s and 1980s, and early music proved to be a testing ground for an emerging musicology of performance. New methodologies of performance analysis, particularly of recordings, did much to reshape an understanding of the contribution of performance to musical meaning, and one of the abiding lessons was that no repertoire is 'innocent'; music is shaped and given meaning in performance and reflects not just the moment when the music was composed but also the prejudices and attitudes of the era in which it was performed. The same is inevitably true of the use of such repertoire in cinema, and in highlighting the role of musical performance in films a historiographical approach provides a valuable perspective. In different ways, HIP informed films such as *The Chronicle of Anna Magdalena Bach* (*Chronik der Anna Magdalena Bach*, Jean-Marie Straub & Danièle Huillet, 1968) and *Tous les matins du monde* (Alain Corneau, 1991), biopics wherein the subject and focus was performance itself. However, to commercial cinema, HIP soon became merely another musical fashion to be used and discarded. It seems unlikely, after all, that HIP was uppermost in the minds of the producers of the Bond movie, *A View to a Kill* (John Glen, 1985), when they opted for Trevor Pinnock and the English Concert's recording of the Four Seasons. Indeed, mainstream film has continued to exploit pastiches and parodies of baroque repertoire, such as the Albinoni Adagio in G minor and Bach's Toccata and Fugue in D minor. Such repertoire takes considerably greater licence with original material, synthesising key stylistic elements and combining them with more modern musical trends. The same can be said of the neo-baroque, a subgenre of minimalism which shared some common ground with HIP, and which is the subject of the final section of this Element. Where HIP broadly recreated the performance circumstances that a composer (supposedly) would have anticipated, effectively clothing the music in period dress, the neo-baroque, particularly the music of Michael Nyman and Philip Glass, rethought baroque music more radically and clothed it in modern dress. Both approaches would play a part in cinema, the latter in a broader range of guises, from period films through eco-politics to the horror film.

1 Baroque Music Before World War Two

It is necessary first to sketch in something of the use of baroque instrumental repertoire in pre-war silent and sound cinema. This will help establish a baseline from which to assess the impact of the Vivaldi revival in particular and also show how such music was deemed to offer a limited and often very specific set of connotative values, many of which still operate in cinema today.

Baroque music features rarely and usually very specifically in silent cinema, though a comment by a musical director of the silent era, Max Winkler, sets Bach amongst other certain composers in a way that suggests the determining factor was the classical canon: 'We began to dismember the great masters. We began to murder the works of Beethoven, Mozart, Grieg, J. S. Bach, Verdi, Bizet, Tchaikovsky and Wagner – everything that wasn't protected by copyright from our pilfering' (Cooke, 2010: 11). A survey of the compendiums and encyclopaedias of cue sheets, however, paints a different picture. Ernö Rapée's *Encyclopaedia of Music for Pictures* lists only two pieces by baroque composers: a Menuet [*sic*] by Handel (in the section, 'Minuets') and his Largo (an arrangement of 'Ombra mai fu' from *Xerxes*), both under the rubric of 'Religious Music' (Rapée, 1925). E. Lang and G. West, in their primer, *Musical Accompaniment of Moving Pictures*, also recommend Handel's Largo (an instance of 'Impressive Moods') and Bach's 'Little Fugue, Gm' (presumably the 'Little Fugue' in G minor, BWV 578) for 'Speed' (Lang & West, 1920). Of the some 3,000 pieces in the second volume of Hans Erdman, Giuseppe Becce and Ludwig Brav's encyclopaedia, the *Thematisches Skalenregister* (thematic catalogue), compiled by Becce alone, most are from the nineteenth and twentieth centuries with 11 pieces by Handel and 14 by Rameau, all of them filed under 'opera excerpts' (Erdmann, Becce & Brav, 1927). There is only one piece by Bach in any of the aforementioned encyclopaedias: the Sinfonia from the beginning of Part II of the *Christmas Oratorio* (BWV 248), which is labelled as 'Hirtenmusik' (Shepherd's Music) in a section entitled 'Pastorella alten Stils. Weihnachten' (Pastorals in the old style. Christmas) in the *Thematisches Skalenregister*. Winkler's reference to

Bach is not, then, representative and marks the composer as an exception to a more general rule of the use of baroque repertoire, premised on his status as a 'great' who stands out from the mainstream, something we will encounter in variant forms later.

We cannot be certain to what extent cinema organists, many of whom had a church training, might have brought baroque repertoire to bear on silent films, not least because Bach was a touchstone of technique and pedagogy for cinema organists. George Tootell, for example, recommends Bach's organ compositions as 'the *only* safe and certain way to gain technical perfection in organ playing' (Tootell, 1927: 53), though it is significant that he is amused and therefore unconvinced by an engineer-mechanic's proposal of Bach's Toccata in F major as a suitable piece for film accompaniment (Tootell, 1927: 10). Tootell does, though, prescribe two pieces by Bach and one by Handel under the heading 'Old Time': a minuet ('stately') from *Berenice* ('The Minuet from *Berenice*'); a Gavotte and a Gigue by Bach (perhaps the Gavotte from Partita for solo violin No. 3 in E major, BWV 1006 and the Gigue from French Suite No. 5 in G major, BWV 816). Winkler claims that '[t]he immortal chorales of J. S. Bach became an "Adagio Lamentoso" for sad scenes', suggesting that what might have been played in church on Sunday was recycled in the cinema on Monday (Cooke, 2010: 11).

Four non-mutually exclusive attitudes to baroque music emerge from this brief survey: first, as a signifier of religion and Christianity ('Christmas music'), an association that presumably derived from attending church services or concerts of religious oratorios; second, an antiquating effect whereby early music connotes a generalised rather than a coeval past ('Old Times'); third, as an expression of dignity and formality, suitable for depictions of the aristocratic world ('stately'); and fourth, the straightforward appeal of a 'good' recognisable tune, more familiar today as a Popular Classic, for example Handel's 'Largo', 'The Minuet from *Berenice*', and so on. What baroque music did *not* do is just as significant: it did not serve as a standard illustration of emotional states – love, grief, jeopardy, amongst others– or provide thematic material deemed suitable for character types – villain, hero, heroine and the like. Consequently, we can venture that baroque music was only occasionally heard in conjunction with silent films.

Nevertheless, some of the repertoire's principles informed the musical taxonomy of silent cinema, at least in Europe. Irene Comisso has argued that there is a direct line from the musico-hermeneutic concept of *Affektenlehre*, and the eighteenth-century principles on which it is based, to the film-music designation of *Stimmungen*. These *Stimmungen*, or moods, were central to the methodology of the first of the two-volume *Allgemeines Handbuch der Film-Musik*, as Irene Comisso explains: 'The *Stimmungen* are … depicted by recourse to metaphors for the emotions such as "agitato" or "mysterious"; these, in turn, correspond to specific musical themes and clichés, here arranged like a hermeneutic code. ... In constructing this "classifying structure", clear reference is made to the music-rhetorical "figures" devised by the *Affektenlehre*' (Comisso, 2012: 98). Maria Fuchs offers support by tracing the personal connections between the two main authors of the *Handbuch*, composers Hans Erdmann and Ludwig Brav, and the musicologist Hermann Kretzschmar who, along with but separately from Hugo Goldschmidt and Arnold Schering, was responsible for the development of a modern interest in the *Affektenlehre* (Fuchs, 2014: 163–4). Fuchs points to the European preference for classifying music according to mood, in contrast to the American preference for programmatic titles (Fuchs, 2014: 161–2). The latter practice earned Erdmann and Becce's scorn, much of which was directed at Ernö Rapée, the New York-based musical director, whose (misleadingly titled) *Motion Picture Moods for Pianists and Organists* and *Encyclopaedia of Music for Pictures*, rather than organising music according to expressive properties, opted for illustrative titles such as Aeroplane, Arabian, Birds, and so on (Rapée, 1924, 1925).[1]

In his survey of the use of Bach in silent film, James M. Doering notes the singular absence of J. S. Bach in the Library of Congress holdings of silent-film music (Doering, 2019). Where the surname did crop up, it more often than not referred to composers of the nineteenth and twentieth centuries rather than the eighteenth. When J. S. Bach made his appearance it was clearly signalled, as in two 'Deluxe Theater' presentations of the silent era, Max Winkler's combinative score for Giulio Antamoro's *Christus* (Doering, 2019: 15) and Hugo Riesenfeld's compilation score of J. S. Bach, Rameau, Vivaldi, Handel and Corelli for Ernst Lubitsch's *Anna Boleyn* (1920) (released as *Deception* in the USA) (Anderson, 1987 and Altman, 2004: 315–16). In both cases, the music was clearly anachronistic and drew instead on different but familiar connotations of religiosity and courtliness respectively. Thereafter, '[a]s the twenties progressed . . . [a] core of three pieces emerged as the essential Bach repertoire: the Bach-Gounod "Ave Maria", the Air on the G String, and the Toccata and Fugue in D Minor' (Doering, 2019: 28).

As silent cinema gave way to the sound era, Bach's Toccata and Fugue in D minor quickly established itself as a horror-film trope (van Elferen, 2012). Its

---

[1] A line of thought from eighteenth-century music through to Kretzschmar, thence to Erdmann and Becce, has been more recently traced in topic theory, thence into film-music theory. For more, see part 3 of Neumeyer (2015, 183–265); and Mirka (2014). Mirka points out that the early twentieth-century reinvention of *Affektenlehre* misrepresents the subjective component admitted by Mattheson. Mattheson did not insist, as Kretzschmar and his followers did, that specific musical affects bore unequivocal meaning.

Grand Guignol opening statement, a gesture like a slashing blade, was used in *Dr Jekyll and Mr Hyde* (Rouben Mamoulian, 1931), *The Black Cat* (Edgar G. Ulmer, 1934) and *The Raven* (Lew Landers, 1935), and has become an abiding signifier of sociopathy more generally (Lerner, 2009 and van Elferen, 2012). Setting aside that the piece might not actually have been written by Bach at all (Williams, 1981), its associations with cinematic horror have become intertwined (exceptions being the abstract interpretations of experimental film-maker Mary Ellen Bute's *Synchromy no. 4: Escape* (1937) and the more mainstream *Fantasia* (Walt Disney, 1940)), cropping up regularly in various knowing guises in *Sunset Boulevard* (Billy Wilder, 1950), *Rollerball* (Norman Jewison, 1975) and *The Babadook* (Jennifer Kent, 2014).

Baroque music in early sound cinema more generally clearly lagged behind such local instances. Surprisingly, despite recognition of him as a 'great master', to use Winkler's term, Bach was not the subject of a biopic during this era, while his contemporary, George Frideric Handel, was accorded the honour in *The Great Mr Handel* (Norman Walker, 1942). That it was made during the war to some extent explains its nationalist orientation, with the composer portrayed as very much the English gentleman rather than a German immigrant, a tension also felt in Handel studies and described as 'the battle for the *Umlaut*' (Mann & Knapp, 1969: 6). That same nationalistic context also motivates the use of the music of Purcell in the Gainsborough production of *The Wicked Lady* (Leslie Arliss, 1945) (and later in extreme contrast in Wendy Carlos's adaptation of the march from the same composer's Music for the Funeral of Queen Mary for *A Clockwork Orange* (Stanley Kubrick, 1971)). *The Wicked Lady*'s deployment of various movements from Purcell's *Abdelazer* suite as diegetic accompaniment in marriage and dance scenes was perhaps determined by the coincidence of its release in 1945 with the 250th anniversary of the death of Henry Purcell (1659–95). Important commem-orative concerts were staged in London in that anniversary year, some of them organised by Michael Tippett, featuring his arrangements of the earlier composer's work together with some by Benjamin Britten (Wiebe, 2012: 77–9). The following year saw the premiere of Britten's *The Young Person's Guide to the Orchestra*, based on the Rondeau from Purcell's *Abdelazer* suite, and a production of *The Fairy Queen* at Covent Garden, the first opera to be staged after the war. Together, this and other interest constituted a Purcell revival. On the continent, though, a rival revival was gathering pace.

2 The Vivaldi Revival

It is difficult today to imagine a world where a seemingly ubiquitous composer like Vivaldi was a relative unknown, yet a review in *The New York Times* of a concert in April 1950 commends the organisers for having 'made at least a step in awakening the local public to the remarkable quantity and quality of Vivaldi's music, so little known to audiences of today' (Downes, 1950). Composers and conductors rediscovering and championing their national forebears is a familiar story and by no means limited to the Purcell revival. Bach had benefited from a similar dynamic in the nineteenth century, ushered in by Johann Nikolaus Forkel's biography and Felix Mendelssohn's performance of the St Matthew Passion in 1829 (Haskell, 1988: 13–16). The same currents were at work in the Vivaldi revival and an agreed and well-documented narrative emerged, one in which Bach would play a minor role (Verona, 1964; Rinaldi, 1978; Abbado, 1979; Nicolodi, 1980; Talbot, 1988; Paul, 2016: 159–98). Despite several of Vivaldi's concertos having been transcribed by Bach and the Italian's influence being noted by Forkel, a general Teutonic disdain for the Italian composer, evident since the eighteenth century, remained. The full weight of retroactive authority began to be felt only after two German musicologists, Julius Rühlmann and Paul Graf Waldersee, independently argued that Bach's transcriptions of Vivaldi were more than technical exercises: they influenced him as well.[2] It was not, though, until the early twentieth century and the publication of Albert Schering's 1905 history of the concerto, *Geschichte des Instrumentalkonzerts*, that Vivaldi's true contribution to music history was recognised. In 1927, Vivaldi was familiar enough to the lay public for Fritz Kreisler to pass off his own Concerto in C in the composer's name. However, if one were looking for a thematic catalogue of Vivaldi's instrumental work at that time, all that was available was an article by Wilhelm Altmann in a musicological journal that accounted only for (most of) the music printed during Vivaldi's lifetime, a hundred or so sonatas and concertos; this from a composer who we now know wrote over 500 concertos alone. There remained a highly significant ingredient to be added to the mix of enthusiastic nationalist entrepreneurism and academic (re-)evaluation: manuscript discovery.

In the late 1920s, a monastic community in Montferrat sent a collection of manuscripts to the Biblioteca Nazionale in Turin, which in turn forwarded them to a professor of music at the University of Milan, Alberto Gentili. Amongst the various papers, Gentili discovered fourteen large volumes of what he recognised as Vivaldi's autograph manuscripts, and subsequent detective work brought to light the other half of the collection. Collectively known as the Turin manuscripts, the collection amounted to several hundred works in various genres – concertos, sonatas, operas, serenatas, motets, sections of the Mass, Psalm settings – as well as sketches and early drafts. As Michael Talbot puts it,

---

[2] Rühlmann (1867), 393–7, 401–5, 413–16; and Waldersee (1885).

'at a stroke Vivaldi cease[d] to be, in practical terms, a "specialist" composer comparable with Corelli and [became] instead a "universal" composer comparable with Handel' (Talbot, 1988: xix). World War II saw the loss of only a few Vivaldi manuscripts and research continued fairly uninterrupted with the publication of two slim monographs by Michelangelo Abbado and Mario Rinaldi, both of whom would, in due course, write the history of the revival (Abbado, 1942; Rinaldi, 1943). A more general interest in Italian baroque repertoire was attested by Marc Pincherle's biography of Corelli (1933, rev. 1954), the first full-length monograph of Tomaso Albinoni, written in 1945 by Remo Giazotto (a character we will encounter later), Pincherle's biography of Vivaldi in 1948 and Franz Giegling's 1949 study of Torelli.[3]

Several professional and semi-professional organisations dedicated to Vivaldi were active before and after the war, the most famous example being the Rapallo concerts staged between 1933 and 1938 by the poet Ezra Pound and the violinist Olga Rudge. Separately, Olga Rudge teamed up with David Nixon, a violinist, to form the Vivaldi Society in Venice, the inaugural concert of which was on 24 March 1938. That enterprise failed, but in its place came the Settimana musicale or 'Vivaldi week' staged between 16 and 21 September 1939, a week of concerts under the direction of the composer Alfredo Casella organised by The Accademia Musicale Chigiana in Siena, which hosted the Centro di Studi Vivaldiani (Adams, 1975: 116). In 1947, the publishers Ricordi, in collaboration with the Treviso-based Istituto Italiano Antonio Vivaldi, founded by Antonio Fanna and the composer Gian Francesco Malipiero, initiated a project with the aim of publishing all of Vivaldi's music. As Manfred Bukofzer noted in his survey of baroque music, until that time '[o]nly a small part of Vivaldi's incredibly prolific production [had] ever been published' (Bukofzer, 1947: 229). The widest dissemination of Vivaldi's work, though, would come from recordings, particularly on the new format of the long-playing record, which within ten years would supplant the til-then industry standard of the shellac 78 rpm. With its longer playing time – over twenty minutes per side rather than five – the LP could accommodate four baroque concertos on a single disc. The new format coincided with the establishment of new orchestras whose slimmed-down forces clarified Vivaldi's contrapuntal complexities: 'Angelo Ephrikian's "Orchestra della Scuola Veneziana" (founded in 1947), Renato Fasano's "Virtuosi di Roma" (1948) and the conductorless ensemble "I Musici" (1952), and similar small chamber groups

---

[3] Giazotto (1945); Pincherle (1948); Giegling (1949). During the 1950s, Pincherle revised and expanded his 1933 biography of Corelli, published as Marc Pincherle (1954), *Corelli et son temps* (Paris: Editions Le Bon Plaisir), translated into English by Hubert E. M. Russell and published in 1956 as *Corelli: His Life, His Work* (New York: W. W. Norton).

formed in France, Britain and the USA' (Talbot, 1988: xx–xxi). Until that time, Vivaldi's music had been shrouded in nineteenth-century orchestrations, illustrated by a concert conducted by Bernardino Molinari at the Basilica of Massenzio that the heroine attends in *Lo Squadrone Bianco* (Augusto Genina, 1936).[4] The performance is of the Largo, the second movement of Vivaldi's Concerto No. 4 in F minor, Op. 8 (RV 297), that is, Winter from the Four Seasons. It is played by a large symphonic orchestra, which includes two full-size harps and grand piano at a sedate 55 bpm (modern performances are around the 75 bpm mark) (Fertonani, 1989). A recording of the Four Seasons, featuring Louis Kaufman as the soloist, won the Grand Prix du Disque in 1950, and while it was Vivaldi's concertos that were to occupy centre stage for some time to come, there was no shortage of other overlooked Italian composers' music to record.[5] Dorottya Fabian observes that 'a large part of [the early-music] movement's activity between the 1950s and the 1970s was still the exploration of the repertoire' and thus, rather like the architects of the *politique des auteurs*, who were swamped by American films banned during the wartime occupation, consumption preceded evaluation (Fabian, 2003: 3–4).

A backlash was not far off. Eleven years later, the journalist and musicologist H. C. Robbins Landon skewered the fashion for all things baroque in a scathing piece published in *High Fidelity* in June 1961, 'A Pox on Manfredini'.[6] It described how, after a period abroad living in Vienna, he returned to a Manhattan where 'you didn't play Mozart quartets on the phonograph, you stacked a pile of LPs on the changer – Albinoni, Geminiani, Corelli, Locatelli, and, of course, the father-figure of barococo music: Antonio Vivaldi'.[7] Such

---

[4] The film can be viewed online at www.dailymotion.com/video/x2ykujx (accessed, 28 December 2020) and the section in question is 00:27:18–00:28:58. Catherine Paul sums up the approach succinctly: 'As Cesare Fertonani has shown, Bernardino Molinari's sumptuous orchestrations (e.g., sixteen first violins) had many personal and modern twists to them, such as his rendition of the continuo by the combination of a harpsichord and an organ, or his rewriting of entire movements. Ultimately, performances of Vivaldi's music made the Venetian composer familiar to audiences, even if that meant adjusting his music to expectations of late nineteenth-century Italian opera audiences' (Paul, 2016: 161).
[5] The recording was made by the American violinist Louis Kaufman with the Concert Hall Society Orchestras, conducted by Henry Swoboda and recorded in Carnegie Hall in 1947. It was first released on the Concert Hall Society Inc. record label as 78 rpm discs in 1948, and subsequently as an LP in 1950 as CHC-1001. An earlier recording of 1942 conducted by Bernardino Molinari with the Rome Augusteo Orchestra had been released on the Parlophone Cetra label in 1942: BB 2043–8.
[6] The reference to Manfredini, hardly a household name and even today warranting only three paragraphs in *Grove Music Online*, may have been used by Landon to suggest a made-up name or because of the homophony with Mantovani, a modern composer forever associated with wall-paper music.
[7] A considered account of this attack and the context of the baroque revival can be found in Fink (2005), 186–297.

calcification into cliché is similarly captured in a scene from 'La Ricotta', Pasolini's satirical contribution to the portmanteau movie, *RoGoPaG* (Roberto Rossellini, Jean-Luc Godard, Pier Paolo Pasolini and Ugo Gregoretti, 1963). The film portrays the making of a biopic of Christ, with a motley cast and crew overseen by Orson Welles as the cynical director. When a *tableau vivant* of the descent from the cross is ready to be filmed (a reconstruction of the Mannerist painter Rosso Fiorentino's *Deposition*, Pinacoteca Comunale, Volterra, oil on wood, c.1521), music is cued. By mistake, a pop song plays. 'Not that one . . . *Publicani!* Blasphemers. The Scarlatti record!' the first assistant director shouts. Along similar lines, at a round-table discussion in 1964 where Pasolini faced a panel of students and faculty of the Centro Sperimentale de Cinematografia, one commentator noted that the use of Bach had become 'somewhat of an affectation' (Pasolini et al., 1965: 39). This, though, is to jump ten years ahead. Before the drift towards cliché through overexposure, the impact of the Vivaldi revival would be felt in the cinema of the early 1950s.

2.1 Melville, Renoir and the Integrationist Approach

It was European and particularly French cinema which initially embraced Vivaldi, the first significant example being *Les Enfants terribles* (Jean-Pierre Melville, 1950). This claustrophobic tale of a quasi-incestuous relationship between a young brother and sister was adapted by Jean-Pierre Melville and Jean Cocteau from the latter's novel of the same name, with the author providing a voice-over.

Paul (Edouard Dermit) is a frail teenager, looked after by his older sister, Elisabeth (Nicole Stéphane), to whom this task falls because their mother is bedridden. When the mother dies, Elisabeth is forced to find work as a model in a dress shop, and befriends Agathe (Renée Cosima), a woman of her own age. Through Agathe, Elisabeth meets Michael (Melvyn Martin), a rich young American, to whom she becomes engaged. The four youngsters, together with Paul and Elisabeth's long-term friend Gérard (Jacques Bernard), move into Michael's house, which Elisabeth inherits outright when her fiancé dies in an automobile accident. Paul falls in love with Agathe and she with him, though both remain unaware of the reciprocity because of Elisabeth's jealous treachery. Love-struck, Paul commits suicide and, as he lies dying, the truth comes out. Elisabeth shoots herself in front of Agathe.

Save for the diegetic performance of 'Were You Smiling At Me' by Melvyn Martin (who plays Michael), the music consists exclusively of concertos by Vivaldi and Bach, and was specially recorded for the film with no subsequent record release. The music track comprises movements and sections of movements from: Vivaldi's Concerto in A minor for two violins and string orchestra (RV 522, which Bach transcribed for organ at Weimar as Concerto in A minor, BWV 593); Vivaldi's Concerto in D minor for violin (RV 813/vclass RV Anh. 10, at one time attributed to Torelli); and Bach's Concerto in A minor for four harpsichords (BWV 1065), adapted from Vivaldi's Concerto in B minor for four violins and cello (RV 580). The last, rather than harpsichords, is played on four pianos, and the piano can be heard prominently as a continuo instrument in the other two concertos.

We do now know the reasons for the choice of specific repertoire – Melville's notes for the film and all his records were destroyed in a fire in 1967 at the Studio Jenner, which he owned. One obvious motivation is the number of solo instruments and of main characters. Vivaldi's concerto for two violins is used twice, once when Elisabeth busies herself with domestic chores, placing items in their 'treasure drawer' and preparing Paul for bed, and later when Paul observes Elisabeth, Agathe, Michael and Gérard from behind a tree (cues 4 and 7). This implies a correspondence between the siblings and the dual instruments and, similarly, the Bach concerto for four harpsichords hints at the complex and incestuous *ménage à quatre* of the four main characters: Paul and Elisabeth, and the naïve victims of Elisabeth's incestuous machinations, Agathe and Gérard. However, the music goes beyond such simple geometry. Both composers are acknowledged in the credit sequence (Figures 1a and 1b):

Judging by his later use of excerpts from Gluck's late-baroque opera *Orfeo ed Euridice* in *Le testament d'Orphée, ou ne me demandez pas pourquoi!* (Jean Cocteau, 1960), one is tempted to credit Cocteau with the choice of music in *Les Enfants terribles*. However, Melville claimed that he was responsible (Anderson, 2013: 233–4 and 277–85; Nogueira, 1971: 42). The director, an insomniac, believed that the editing room was the place where a film was really made, and he spent many of his nights there, which helps explain the film's taut interlacing of musical and filmic detail. A broader musical awareness is also evident, perhaps thanks to the contribution of a musical advisor. For example, the siren that Paul and Gérard hear when travelling to Paul's home from school (0:08:50) oscillates between G♯ and A, the sharpened leading note and tonic of the most-used key in the film, A minor. And all cues end in A major or its most obvious variants: A minor, the dominant or subdominant (E and D), or the relative major, C.

Theorists have acknowledged the role of music in the film, though few have analysed it in detail. Noël Burch, writing just two years after its release, addressed the rationale for the music and also considered its style. Rejecting

(a)

(b)

Figures 1a and 1b Opening credit sequence of *Les Enfants terribles* (reproduced by kind permission of Carole Weisweiller)

romantic and neo-romantic atonal and dodecaphonic music on the grounds that such repertoire would merely repeat an element already present in the film, he approves Vivaldi's music as a vehicle for the analytic dimension of the original novel: 'the music provides, in an impartial and almost mathematical manner, the commentative, analytic aspect of the work' (Burch, 1952: 6).[8] Burch draws on familiar tropes of baroque music – its self-governing musical forms, its detachment and its mathematicity – and Edward Baron Turk takes a similar view, arguing that 'complex patterns of florid counterpoint [and] the rapports of symmetry, opposition, and repetition inherent in baroque polyphonic music serve as the perfect auditory complement' (Turk, 1980: 30). 'Devoid of specific dramatic expression', baroque counterpoint thus reiterates the various characters' stratagems and is significantly absent 'during the sequences in which Elisabeth pretends to seek out a more normal life' (Turk, 1980: 29–30). This echoes Burch's observation that the music is absent in the scenes set in Nice, which he describes as 'comédie mondaine'. Burch, though, allows for the

---

[8] ' . . . c'est la musique qui commente d'une manière impartiale et presque mathématique tout [le côté analytique] de l'oeuvre'. All translations are my own unless otherwise stated.

Table 1 List of musical cues and action in *Les Enfants terribles* *

Cue	Timing	Music used (final chord of cue)	Action
1.	0:29–2:44:	Vivaldi, Concerto for violin in D minor (RV 813). Last movement: *Allegro*. Bars 1–64 + last two bars. (A minor)	The credits over a virtual silhouette of Elisabeth who stands over Paul, lying on a billiard table beneath a tree, an image encountered later in Elisabeth's dream.
2.	3:10–5:16	Bach, Concerto for four harpsichords in A minor (BWV 1065). First movement: *Allegro moderato*. Bars 48–103 (i.e. end of the movement). (A minor)	School ends and the pupils have a snowball fight, which ends when Paul is knocked out.
3.	9:12–9:47	Bach, Concerto for four harpsichords in A minor (BWV 1065). Last movement: *Allegro*. Bars 104–123 (end of movement). (A minor)	Paul and Gérard arrive at Paul's apartment block and mount the stairs to his apartment.
4.	13:02–15:00	Vivaldi, Concerto for two violins in A minor (Op. 3, No. 8; RV 522). First movement, *Allegro*. Bars 1–55 (fade out, A)	Elisabeth busies herself with domestic chores and gets Paul back into bed.
5.	23:55–24:58	Bach, Concerto for four harpsichords in A minor (BWV 1065). Second movement: *Largo* section. Bars 1–10 (second beat). (C)	Paul's first sleepwalking episode, observed by Elisabeth.

Table 1 (cont.)

Cue	Timing	Music used (final chord of cue)	Action
6.	40:16–40:48	Bach, Concerto for four harpsichords in A minor (BWV 1065). First movement, *Allegro moderato*. Third beat of 12 to downbeat of 28. (A minor)	Gérard steals a watering can and runs off, followed by Paul and Elisabeth.
7.	55:59–56:29	Vivaldi, Concerto for two violins in A minor (Op. 3, No. 8; RV 522). First movement: *Allegro*. Halfway through bar 75 to halfway through 88. (fade out, E minor 7)	From behind a tree, Paul observes Elisabeth and Agathe meeting Gérard and Michael. The four of them drive off in Michael's car.
8.	1:01:58–1:02:23	Vivaldi, Concerto for violin in D minor (RV 813). Last movement: *Allegro*. Bars 1–halfway through 12. (A minor)	Paul, Elisabeth, Gérard, Agathe and Michael tour Michael's house.
9.	1:08:25–1:10:42	Bach, Concerto for four harpsichords in A minor (BWV 1065). Second movement: *Più grave section*, complete. Bars 11–35. (E)	Paul discovers his new lair.
10.	1:12:12–1:14:09	Bach, Concerto for four harpsichords in A minor (BWV 1065). Second movement, *Più grave section*. Bars 11–32, i.e. orchestra chord. (fade out, E7)	Paul and Elisabeth talk in his lair.
11.	1:17:48–1:18:56	Vivaldi, Concerto for violin in D minor (RV 813). Last movement: *Allegro*. Bars 12–47. (A)	Elisabeth leaves Agathe and goes to visit Paul and encounters Gérard on the stairs.
12.	1:21:16–1:22:40	Bach, Concerto for four harpsichords in A minor (BWV 1065). Second movement: *Largo section*, complete. Bars 1–15. (E)	Elisabeth finds a letter and reads it (contents supplied by voice-over). She disposes of the letter.

13.	1:25:14–1:25:40	Bach, Concerto for four harpsichords in A minor (BWV 1065). Second movement, Più grave section. Bars 1–halfway through 5. (D minor(maj7))	Cocteau voice-over as Elisabeth walks from Paul's lair back to her room.
14.	1:28:21–1:29:54	Bach, Concerto for four harpsichords in A minor (BWV 1065). Second movement, *Più grave* section. Halfway through bar 5–32. (fade out, E7)	Elisabeth sees Paul sleepwalking. She follows him and finds herself at a washbasin where she washes her hands. ('Her eyes cast down, Elisabeth washed her appalling hands.') Paul is dying.
15.	1:37:47–1:38:55	Bach, Concerto for four harpsichords in A minor (BWV 1065): Second movement: Più grave section. Bars 12–32. (quick fade on chord of E7)	
16.	1:39:47–1:41:14	Bach, Concerto for four harpsichords in A minor (BWV 1065). Second movement: Più grave section, bars 8–32. (E7)	Elisabeth's final speech with fantasy sequence. Paul dies.
17.	1:41:32–1:41:57	Vivaldi, Concerto for violin in D minor (RV 813). Last movement: Allegro. Bars 57–64 + last two bars. (A minor)	Elisabeth shoots herself.

* All timings from *Les Enfants terribles* (Jean-Pierre Melville, 1950), British Film Institute, BFIVD634, DVD.

music's more affective contribution, arguing that it expresses the 'Genius of the Room', 'a type of metaphysical power born of the children's' imaginary world which ends up overpowering them and leading them towards death' (Burch, 1952: 8).[9] Turk's analysis ignores these affective properties and makes music merely a formal correlate, disengaged from the emotional drama. The implication that such music is only about itself serves his reading well, in that the music's intricate surface design can be allied to Elisabeth's calculated plotting. However, it overlooks musical performance and promotes a view that baroque music is all the same, an exercise in musical style with no immanent or potential meaning. Laura Anderson offers a more nuanced view of the relationship between musical style and narrative design. Like Burch, she argues that the music functions both as a distanced commentary and as a metaphoric extension of the drama, but she also allows for Turk's case: 'it is the regular and mechanical rhythms of the Baroque music that help to communicate [Elisabeth's unconscious drive]' (Anderson, 2021: unpaginated). She goes further than both writers, though, pointing to music's agential role, which is allied to Cocteau's voice-over. Music 'often seems detached from the action at hand in the same way that Cocteau as narrator stands apart [which] ensures that, sonically, we experience *Enfants* as a work indelibly linked to Cocteau' (Anderson, 2021: unpaginated). Anderson here proposes a variant model of Claudia Gorbman's *auteur mélomane*, where music is tied to an enunciative source, be it author or director, an issue to which I will return (Gorbman, 2007).

An image of baroque music as merely a formal exercise, a sort of eighteenth-century vamp-till-ready, is a familiar one, particularly in film-music studies. Mervyn Cooke, for example, notes that the music of Bach often serves as 'neutral continuity' (Cooke, 2008: 452) and David Neumeyer traces the 'neutral or stable topical importations' in various cinematic iterations of Bach's Preludes in C and G major (Neumeyer, 2015: 201). Cooke and Neumeyer, though, do not believe that music is ever entirely neutral. As Wye Jamison Allanbrook puts it, 'No moment is ever "expressively neutral": when it ceases to be A, it must be B or C or D' (Allanbrook, 2002: 214). But one instinctively understands what Cooke and Neumeyer mean and the unstated premise from which Turk's reading proceeds: baroque music sits closer to the non-signifying end of an imaginary axis, at the other extreme of which lies more potently semantic music.

That characterisation of baroque repertoire as meaninglessly uniform is encapsulated in the derogatory notion of 'sewing-machine' music that pervaded

---

[9] 'Génie de la chambre', 'espèce de force métaphysique issue du monde imaginaire des enfants qui finit par les dominer et les mener à la mort.'

music criticism in the 1930s and was often ascribed to Arnold Bax.[10] The term was taken up more specifically by Lawrence Dreyfus and Richard Taruskin in seminal essays (Dreyfus, 1983 and Taruskin, 1988) to describe a mode of performance style the 'basic assumptions' of which were 'strong downbeats and "motor rhythms"' (Fabian, 2003: 169). This dated mode of modern baroque music performance encouraged a sense of musical solipsism. Arpeggiation and scalar patterns, which already entailed lower-level predictability, were organised by terraced dynamics which thereby emphasised higher-level inevitability. Furthermore, the interlocking designs of the sequence and the fugue, the latter perhaps the defining baroque compositional technique, elevated such consequential mechanics to the level of self-governing musical determinism. The image of musical solipsism, which still casts its shadow in film-music studies today, was perhaps exacerbated by the rise of the LP, a physically disengaged communion with performance (Pierre Schaeffer's acousmatic listening)

---

[10] The original term is commonly attributed to Arnold Bax, who had a low opinion of Bach. '"Sewing-machine music", said Arnold of Bach's suites (he did not object to the later Preludes and Fugues, it seemed)' (Cohen, 1969: 46). A review by W. J. Turner in the *Illustrated London News* on 17 September 1932 of a Promenade concert entirely of Bach at the Queen's Hall provides this withering observation: 'I nearly always get the impression on these Bach evenings that the soloists and the orchestra have been turned into musical sewing-machines, executing their musical stitches automatically and regularly. But not machines of a very advanced type, not Rolls-Royces, or supercharged Mercedes, but mere honest-to-goodness, stock sewing-machines'. In that same year, a review in *The Times* cited Bax: *The Times*, 13 August 1932: 6: 'Was it not Mr. Arnold Bax who once irreverently spoke of "the sewing-machine rhythm" of J. S. Bach? Whether it were he or another everyone was properly shocked; yet somehow the phrase sticks, and it is apt to come back to mind when one listens to Bach at a Promenade Concert. Those whirring groups of semiquavers with an accent on the first of every four seem to be sewing their unerring seam in a garment of more utility than beauty.' Bax's surprising disdain for Bach's music is referred to by Aloys Fleischmann in a radio interview with Michael Oliver: Richard Adams, '"The Golden Age Has Passed" – a Radio Documentary on Bax by Michael Oliver', YouTube (22 February 2020), www.youtube.com/watch?v=XWTu8rx2YYM&t=316s at 47:00.

  Lawrence Dreyfus uses the term to describe the performance mode associated with the Vivaldi revival – roughly 1945–60 – and provides a summary of its key features: 'the period of the "sewing-machine" style, sometimes called the "Vivaldi revival", [was] when German chamber orchestras enthusiastically took up "terraced dynamics", when historically minded conductors urged players to stop "phrasing", and when repeat signs in the music occasioned a blaze of premeditated embellishments. "Motoric rhythms", it seemed, revealed a new species of musical gratification – the freedom from feeling' (Dreyfus, 1983: 303). Writing shortly after Dreyfus, Richard Taruskin widened the historical period when considering five recordings made between 1935 and 1985, and argued that they all bore the same hallmarks. This was part of Taruskin's more general argument that performance of all music was influenced by modernist aesthetics, producing an objective or 'geometric' style as opposed to a 'vitalist' approach (Taruskin, 1988). In so doing, he flattened the distinction between recordings from the early and later parts of the twentieth century, on which point Fabian quite rightly challenges him. She argues that in some cases the HIP style challenge to the mainstream performance style (MSP) produced performances that '[made] the music "speak" as a good orator would using the conventions and classical art of rhetoric. This approach and aesthetics foster rhythmic flexibility and localized rubato, dynamic inflections, free ornamentation and other expressive liberties' (Fabian, 2015: 30).

combined with a perceived mode of inexpressivity. Anahid Kassabian, for example, lists the characteristics of baroque music as 'intricacy, excess, ornamentation, restraint, calculation, and lack of emotion' (Kassabian, 2001: 70), a virtual inventory of the terms that Turk employs. Add to this frequent references to the repertoire's mathematicity and it is easy to see why the notion of abstraction is never far away. Note here that Cooke talks of 'the *abstract* use of baroque music in Jean-Pierre Melville's Cocteau tale *Les Enfants terribles*', a term which he later employs about Bach's music, 'the most inherently abstract in conception of any classical style to have featured prominently in the movies' (Cooke, 2008: 434, my emphasis, and 448).

Regrettably, a notion of neutrality discourages the search for significance and dissuades the film theorist from examining more subtle correspondences between film and musical rhythm. Instead, the presumption that baroque music, compared to repertoire whose more deliberate musico-rhetorical gestures suggest emotional states, abides; the music is not braided with the drama but treads its own path, indifferent to the images to which it is yoked. In Turk's case, neutrality represents disinterest and is a *tabula rasa* upon which his reading of the film can be superimposed. Music becomes an ironic metaphorisation of 'ineluctable destiny' (Turk, 1980: 30), the churning clockwork inevitability of baroque musical design, paralleling narrative teleology. Baroque music is thus a signifier of faceless determinism and/or Elisabeth's plotting, a view advanced by Turk, Anderson and also by Ginette Vincendeau: 'The music … has a sinister, hypnotic function when it seemingly drives Elisabeth along, like an automaton, on her deadly machinations between Paul and Agathe' (Vincendeau, 2003: 34). Vincendeau is sensitive to Melville's careful editorial strategies: 'Bach and Vivaldi's relentless rhythm gives these scenes a fateful quality, to which Melville appears to choreograph both characters' movements and editing' (Vincendeau, 2003: 34).

Vincendeau does not elaborate, but it is possible to point to several moments when character movement, musical rhythm and film editing are closely entwined. On three occasions, rising sequences accompany characters as they climb stairs: when Paul and Gérard approach Paul's apartment (Bach BWV 1065: bars 114–21, 09:30–09:38); when Michael shows his new friends his house (Vivaldi RV 813, final movement: bars 8–10, 1:02:12–1:02:20); and when Elisabeth mounts the stairs later (same music: 1:18:36–1:18:32). Though the last cues are preceded by a descending sequence, the alignment of physical and musical ascension suggests more than coincidence (although this is admittedly plausible, given the frequency of rising sequences in this repertoire). Furthermore, in the first of these cues the final chord ends exactly as Paul and Gérard arrive at the front door to ring the bell. Similar tight calibration between music and act in the form of a stinger occurs when Paul is knocked out by the snowball/stone. The arrival and departure of music usually observes musical form. However, on occasion the music is faded, and more often than not such fades are synchronised with optical equivalents. For example, the ripieno entry on a chord of E7 at bar 32 of the Più grave section of Bach's BWV 1065 coincides with a wipe from Paul's exploration of his new room to him in bed later. This occasional use of acoustic fades suggests that the music was recorded in complete sections rather than as a series of separate cues. Furthermore, it seems likely that Melville had some input in terms of appropriate tempi and mood, and that Paul Bonneau, the musical director (married at the time to Jacqueline Bonneau, one of the pianists involved in the recording) was closely involved in both pre- and post-production.[11] Such attention to detail is also found in the use of the Più grave and Largo of Bach's Concerto BWV 1065, cues which underline the relevance of performance practice to any study of early-music repertoire in cinema. Both are played on pianos at a startlingly slow tempo, relative, that is, to more recent interpretations, reflecting performance practice of the post-war era. A 1948 recording of the Bach concerto, for example, also played on four pianos, is marginally slower than the version conducted by Paul Bonneau for the film.[12] In short, given the history of recording styles, it would have been quite difficult for Melville to have imagined Bach differently from the way it sounds in *Les Enfants terribles*. That is particularly true of the Più grave, which sounds more like a Chopin piano prelude than eighteenth-century repertoire.[13] Contrary motion (in both

---

[11] Paul Bonneau (1918–95) was a composer and conductor active in light music and film. Jacqueline Bonneau, née Pangnier (1917–2007), though using the professional name Jacqueline Robin, was a pianist and accompanist, noted for her work with the French bass-baritone, Gérard Souzay (1918–2004) and the Greek mezzo soprano Irma Kolassi (1918–2012) on German lieder in particular. She was part of a celebrated duo-piano partnership with Geneviève Joy (1919–2009), who was also one of the piano soloists for *Les Enfants terribles*. Arguably the most famous of the four pianists was Éliane Richepin (1910–99). The fourth pianist was André Collard (1911–?). None of the performers or the conductor appear to have had any profile as a baroque specialist.

[12] In the film, the quaver pulse of the Largo is around 75 bpm, compared to 72 bpm in *J. S. Bach Concerto for Three Pianos (C Major) and Concerto for Four Pianos (A Minor)* by The Pro Musica Chamber Orchestra conducted by Arthur Goldschmidt with Gisèle Kühn, Georgette Astorg, Guy Lasson and C. Beche, Polydor PLP 6650 (1948) LP.

[13] The tempo for the Più grave is almost half of that employed by Ton Koopman, Trevor Pinnock and Christopher Hogwood in their recordings. A crotchet pulse obtains in all of them – Koopman 63 bpm, Pinnock 75 bpm and Hogwood 69 bpm – while the recording in the film is difficult to hear as anything other than a succession of quavers at 75 bpm. The same applies to the Largo. In the film, a quaver is roughly 59 bpm, while for Koopman, a crotchet is 65 bpm, for Pinnock 57 bpm and 61 bpm for Hogwood. *J. S. Bach: Harpsichord Concertos, BWV 1060–1062 & 1065*, Amsterdam Baroque Orchestra with Ton Koopman, Tini Mathot, Elina Mustonen and Patrizia Marisaldi, Erato-Elatus 2292-45649-2 (November 1988), CD; *Bach: Concertos for 3 & 4 Harpsichords*, the English Concert with Trevor Pinnock, Kenneth Gilbert, Lars Ulrik

movements) and terraced rhythms, features that otherwise delineate the individual lines, are lost in the softly blurred articulation of modern instruments, and it is harmonic structure rather than local rhythms that produce in the listener an awareness of broader metrical organisation. The net effect is of a hazy wash of sound.

One can describe the performances as inexpressive in so far as, with little to distinguish the separate contributions of the four pianos, individuality is damped down in service of the collective. However, both the Più grave and the Largo are unquestionably affective or, more colloquially, romantic. In part that is due to the nature of baroque slow movements more generally, wherein longer notes encourage expressivity, and chromaticism is more likely to be encountered, features that are sometimes overlooked or downplayed in discussions of baroque performance style. (The 'sewing-machine' style really only applies to fast movements, as Dorottya Fabian's comprehensive studies have highlighted (Fabian, 2003 and 2015).)[14] Modern performance practice, with the leaner profile of gut strings and sharply decaying harpsichords, combined with faster tempi, would not so readily have provided such pliantly associative elucidation of the characters' dark psychopathology. In this light, it is difficult to accept Burch's argument that the music is commentative. Such a view appears to spring not so much from listening to the music but from the image of baroque repertoire as self-involved and thus ineluctably isolated. As we will see in the later section on films that adopt a dissociative approach to baroque music, although *Les Enfants terribles*, like many of those films, has a contemporary setting, music here is used empathetically in the first instance (and the Chopin-like Più grave of BWV 1065 is a case in point).

To consider both movements in more detail, the Più grave is used six times, more than any other cue in the film, and always as consecutive pairs. (The distinct structural organisation of these three pairs of musical cues also applies to the use of the Allegro from Vivaldi's Concerto in D minor for violin, RV 813). Cue 13 begins exactly where cue 9 ended, that is in bar 12, recalling the earlier more optimistic image of the five children touring Michael's house, a place that has now become the setting for Elisabeth's deranged plotting. The first time it is heard, the Più grave cue accompanies Paul's slow and aimless movement through the house (cue 9, Figures 2a and 2b) and, almost immediately, becomes an expression of the wonder

---

Mortensen and Nicholas Kramer, Archiv Productions 400041–2 (February 1981), CD; *J. S. Bach: Concertos for 3 & 4 Harpsichords*, The Academy of Ancient Music with Christopher Hogwood, Davitt Moroney, Christophe Rousset and Colin Tilney, L'Oiseau-Lyre, 433 053–2 (August 1989), CD.

14 Fabian notes that the average tempo of the slow movements of the Brandenburg Concertos increases across the period 1947–82, yet the variation of tempi is considerably greater than that of the fast movements. See Fabian (2003), 115–20.

Figures 2a and 2b (a) Musical miasma; cue 9. Transcription of Più grave. Bach Concerto for four harpsichords (BWV 1065); (b) Paul explores his new lair (reproduced by kind permission of Carole Weisweiller)

of his newly discovered abode, confirmed when Elisabeth, casting an appreciative look around, comments that Paul was lucky to discover it (cue 10).

Cue 13 accompanies a high overhead shot of Elisabeth retracing the route Paul took in cue 9, '[p]rowling like a spider in the darkness, [spinning] her glittering web through the night', as Cocteau's voice-over tells us. While the 'spinning' metaphor, echoed by the music's filigree texture, endorses fate-oriented interpretations, a closer investigation reveals a more careful musical design. Cue 13 fades on an arpeggiated chord of D minor (maj7), and cue 14, which follows some three minutes later, begins from that point. Cue 14 plays to the end of the movement where the final chord of E7 functions as a 'stinger', following unexpectedly from the previous bar's chord of D7, synchronised with Elisabeth plunging her hands beneath the tap in the washbasin, a futile act of ablution that 'all the perfumes of Arabia will not sweeten'. Set in Paul's lair, cues 15 and 16 repeat most of the same musical material and once again utilise the final chord of E7 as stingers: in cue 15, when Agathe grabs Elisabeth by the wrist, and in cue 16 when Paul finally dies. In the case of the Largo from the same Bach concerto, the misty articulation of the pianos and the slow tempo provide a similar opportunity for musico-filmic correspondence (Figure 3).[15]

The solemn opening chords announce in dramatic fashion the first of Paul's sleepwalking episodes (cue 5) and the languidly rendered contrary motion, a feature that Bach added to Vivaldi's otherwise single rising lines, provides a suitably drowsy acoustic analogue of somnambulation. Cue 12 similarly exploits the more melodramatic elements of the movement's crashing chords when Elisabeth discovers and reads Paul's letter, while the extended cadence provides a suitable supplement to her disposal of the letter.

It is clear that baroque music fulfils many different functions in *Les Enfants terribles*. The repertoire itself is far from being inexpressive and, when deftly applied, its potential affects can enhance drama and the moving image. In such light, Melville's contribution is significant and prescient, though the potential of baroque music as music for film that he demonstrated was appreciated by few.[16] Such sensitivity to musical material was not apparent in a marriage of baroque music and cinema that followed two years later in a sonorisation of Carl

Figure 3 Transcription of opening bars of Largo. Bach Concerto for four harpsichords (BWV 1065)

---

[15] Again, more recent recordings are taken at almost double the speed. In the film, a quaver is roughly 59 bpm, while in Pinnock's performance the crotchet is 57 bpm, as compared to 61 bpm for Hogwood and 65 bpm for Koopman.

[16] An exception was François Truffaut. 'When Truffaut was a novice film-maker, he was nice enough to tell me he had seen the film twenty-five times. He proved he knew it even better than I did. He not only knew the words but the music which went with them' (Nogueira, 1971), 47.

Theodor Dreyer's silent film, *La Passion de Jeanne d'Arc* (1928), something of a throwback to the deluxe presentations of the silent era. It was created by Lo Duca, an Italian-born film historian and one of the founding editors of *Cahiers du Cinéma* (for considerably more detail on the history of the film's production and the issues it raises, see Greig, 2020b). The first negative of Dreyer's film had been destroyed by fire in 1928, and in 1929 a second, assembled by Dreyer and his editor from alternate takes, suffered the same fate, meaning that there was no longer a definitive print. In 1951, rummaging through the Paramount vaults in Gennevilliers in Paris, Lo Duca discovered a 16mm version of the second edit. He struck a new print and premiered it at a small independent cinema in March 1952 with music by J. S. Bach, Albinoni, Vivaldi, Palestrina, Beethoven and César Franck, played from a wire recorder. Later that same year, Lo Duca produced a sonorised print for the Venice Biennale, which subsequently went on general release. Lo Duca made several changes to Dreyer's original print, which later critics and Dreyer himself condemned. Despite this, until 1989 when it was withdrawn from circulation, this sonorised version was the most readily available print of a film that regularly appeared in all-time top ten film lists. Exhibitors could turn the music off, as David Bordwell advised (Bordwell, 1973: 79), though that would have thrown into question the long introductory section from which Lo Duca had removed the explanatory intertitles and for which he compensated with a voice-over. Either way, in all likelihood it was this print that directors like Pier Paolo Pasolini, Andrei Tarkovskij and Ingmar Bergman, who counted it amongst their favourite films, would have encountered. Potentially, then, this version of Dreyer's film, 'immersed' in (mainly Italian) baroque music, influenced and consolidated the image of baroque music as a signifier of a generalised past.[17] The music of the print version was by Albinoni, Francesco Geminiani, Giuseppe Torelli, Giovanni Sammartini and, of course, Vivaldi, signalling the influence of the Vivaldi revival and the widening interest in other Italian baroque composers. To this repertoire, Lo Duca added three Bach organ preludes, two brief improvised organ interludes, a snippet of plainsong and sections of Alessandro Scarlatti's *Passio, Domini nostri Jesu Christi secundum Ioannem* (St John Passion). Of these, the organ pieces and the Passion were recorded in Paris specifically for the film.

Lo Duca's approach to the music can easily be gleaned; he separated out the various movements of the concertos and sinfonias and applied them according to what he determined was the dominant emotional tenor of each scene. The slow movements are used mainly to invoke empathy, and the faster movements

---

[17] Lo Duca uses the specific word 'immerse' in Lo Duca (1949): 423; and in Lo Duca (1952): 62.

accompany action or personal confrontation. Lo Duca appears to have determined when certain cues should begin but, with little or no editing of the individual concerto and sinfonia movements, scenes will end and the music continue into the next dramatic sequence. For example, he ignores the new location of the torture chamber, which marks the beginning of Act 3, indicated in the original scripts as such and with an intertitle that he removed, and the Albinoni Adagio in G minor, which accompanies the previous scene, continues fully a minute into the new one. Similarly, he furnishes Act 4 with a new intertitle and once again avoids the obvious synchronisation by having the music, Sinfonia in G major by Sammartini, enter some ten seconds earlier. Synchronisations between music and drama are haphazard and so accidental that it is impossible to argue for the kind of careful local design manifest in *Les Enfants terribles*.

This raises the question of Lo Duca's reasons for choosing the specific repertoire. A correspondence between Lo Duca and Dreyer sees the former suggesting the singular use of Bach's music and the latter approving; the equation of a 'classic' composer with a 'classic' film cannot be discounted. But the main motivation here is surely the sustained evocations of antiquity and religion which had proved such lasting properties of baroque repertoire since the silent era, and which served to amplify a medieval trial that takes place in an ecclesiastical setting. Though Joan had died over 250 years before Bach was born, anachronism had not proven an impediment before and wouldn't again. Baroque music, the reasoning presumably went, sounded old to the modern ear and was idiomatically sufficiently different and unfamiliar enough to serve its intended purpose.

The presence of Albinoni's Adagio in G minor, which takes pride of place in the opening credit sequence and thereafter produces sympathy for Jeanne, provides a more interesting clue to the choice of specific repertoire. The piece was, in fact, a fake, written in the 1940s by Remo Giazotto, a musicologist and author of the first book on the Venetian composer.[18] It was a pastiche very much of its time, which is to say that its design in many ways exemplifies the mode of performance practice of slow movements of baroque instrumental music in the 1950s – languid tempi, lush strings. While the opening shows an obvious debt to the sequential descending string line of Bach's 'Air on a G String', the harmony is pilfered from the first few bars of the first movement of Beethoven's Piano Sonata no. 14 in C-sharp minor (the Moonlight Sonata), and it is Romanticism

---

[18] Giazotto claimed to have discovered two fragments in a library in Dresden in 1945 and reconstructed the Adagio from them, though later quietly dropped the claim. 'Its style is so totally unlike Albinoni's that it invites us to explore his music under false premises' (Talbot, 1994: iii. See also Lugert & Schütz, 1998).

that ultimately wins out. Indeed, it is difficult to imagine how its later, memorable unison string gesture might sound on original instruments (Figure 4), which might explain why no one has tried it.

This dramatic gesture recalls the *Sturm und Drang* opening of Bach's Toccata and Fugue in D minor, and, if we accept Peter Williams' argument that the piece was at some point adapted for organ from its original form as a solo violin piece, it is a composition that similarly benefits from timbral translation (Williams, 1981). The bogus status of the Albinoni aside, it was certainly perceived at the time (and often is now) as an example of baroque music. Lo Duca and the original French audience would have been familiar with it as the signature tune for a popular weekly music programme, *Sinfonia Sacra*, presented by Carl De Nys and Jean Witold. Witold was also the director of L'Ensemble Instrumental 'Sinfonia' and may have been prompted to record the Adagio to exploit the movement's new popularity. Either way, the result was two LPs released on the Éditions Phonographiques Parisiennes dedicated mainly to Albinoni, with the Adagio as the first album's first track. Lo Duca followed suit and all of the instrumental baroque repertoire used in his sonorisation comes from those two LPs, presumably through a lease arrangement with the record company. Lo Duca may have decided to jettison his original more eclectic choices from the March 1952 premiere in favour of Italian musical baroque more generally, which, because of the Vivaldi revival, was very much 'in the air'. His motivation was thus both expedient and pragmatic: expedient because it drew on musical trends; pragmatic because there was an available recorded source. But therein lay a problem. Whether or not Lo Duca was deliberately trying to emulate the cue-sheet system of the silent era or that period's deluxe

Figure 4 Transcription of Giazotto/Albinoni Adagio in G minor, bars 86–9

presentations, pre-recorded music afforded him none of the flexibility that an experienced musical director would otherwise have brought to live performance.

A more polished approach than Lo Duca's loose cut-and-paste process is *The Golden Coach* (Jean Renoir, 1952). Adapted from Prosper Mérimée's play *Le Carrosse du Saint-Sacrement* and released some two years after *Les Enfants terribles*, it is considerably different in tone and ambition to Melville's film and advances Vivaldi's music to a co-starring rather than a supporting role.

At some indeterminate period in the eighteenth century, a troupe of *commedia dell'arte* players led by Don Antonio (Edoardo Spadaro) arrives in a small Peruvian town. At the same time, the Viceroy of the region, Ferdinand (Duncan Lamont), takes delivery of a golden coach. The troupe stage a production for the local people, attended by the local toreador, Ramon (Ricardo Rioli), who is immediately smitten with the leading lady, Camilla (Anna Magnani). The Viceroy commands a private performance at the palace and he too falls under her spell, giving her a beautiful necklace, much to the annoyance of the Viceroy's mistress, the Marquise (Gisella Mathews). Similarly peeved, Camilla's lover, Felipe (Paul Campbell), leaves her to fight a war elsewhere in Peru. As Camilla and the Viceroy's relationship develops, the latter makes a gift to her of the golden carriage. Offended, the nobility threaten to remove him from office, forcing the Viceroy to relent, much to the annoyance of Camilla, who takes up with Ramon again. Felipe returns from the war and learns of Camilla's behaviour. He duels with Ramon and both suitors are arrested. Meanwhile, the Viceroy changes his mind and gives Camilla the coach. In a gesture forced on her by the situation, Camilla donates the carriage to the church and order is restored.

The film was produced by the Panaria Company, a small organisation that until then had made only one film, *Vulcano* (William Dieterle, 1950), also starring Magnani (Bergstrom, 2009: 276–8). The first choice for Panaria's second production, *The Golden Coach*, was Luchino Visconti, but after producing a 'virulently anti-clerical' script and refusing to compromise, Visconti was sacked (Bergstrom, 2009: 278). Approaches were made to Jean Renoir, then living in Hollywood, and he expressed interest. He was keen to return to Europe and wanted to make a film in colour (*The Golden Coach* was eventually shot in Technicolor). Filming took place in Italy with dialogue delivered in English using direct sound, the latter an exception in a country where dubbing was common practice and standard for films made at Cinecittà, which lay directly under the approach to Rome airport. The film would later be post-synched with Italian and French dialogue, though Renoir preferred the English-language version.

Renoir was interested in working with Magnani, but Vivaldi was the more significant muse (Bergstrom, 2009: 280, and Renoir, 1990: 41). 'I bought all the Vivaldi records I could find. There was a composer at the Panaria Company who generally took care of the music in the company's films, and I asked him to help me get to know Vivaldi better' (Renoir, 1990: 42). Such enthusiasm appears to be genuine; this is not the breathless prose of a press release but a considered response two years after the film had been released to Jacques Rivette and François Truffaut, who were then rising film critics.[19] Renoir was also clearly intrigued by the sense of historical discovery that Vivaldi's music presented: 'You know, Vivaldi is still unknown, his manuscripts are being discovered every day' (Renoir, 1990: 42). The spirit of revivalism is also evident in the sleeve notes of the soundtrack release, which carry the (false) claim that '[t]he film marks the first use of [Vivaldi's] music in the cinematic medium'.[20]

The musical director and conductor credited with researching and arranging the music was Gino Marinuzzi Jr. (1920–96). The final selection included contributions from Corelli and Martini, and traditional music of the *commedia dell'arte*, though it is not clear if the composer at the Panaria Company to whom Renoir referred was Marinuzzi. Marinuzzi was an interesting figure, active in the theatre, television, radio and film, a composer of electronic music, a teacher, and the inventor of the Fonosynth, a handheld synthesiser (Corbella, 2015). He had scored his first film, *Romanzo d'amore* (Duilio Coletti), in 1950 and was a joint contributor to an chapter in a notable book on film music, *La musica nel film* (Masetti, 1950). The essay is something of a manifesto and one passage is worth quoting in full:

> What I firmly disagree with is subduing music to the silliest details, to those famous 'secondary syncs' which are not only meaningless, but generate a sense of annoyance in the spectators, who are obliged to listen, in the space of 30 seconds, to an orchestra producing passionate phrases abruptly interrupted by a villain's ambush, followed immediately by a coach leaving, a father crying, a fight, a landscape, etc. ... The composer has become something like a professional 'food taster', who picks at a little of everything and, eventually, eats nothing. (cited in Corbella, 2015: 103, his translation. Originally Masetti, 1950: 36–7)[21]

[19] First published in *Cahiers du Cinéma*, 34 and 35 (1954).
[20] MGM Records E-3111, released 1954 as *Selections from the Sound-Track of 'The Golden Coach'* with the Rome Symphony Orchestra.
[21] 'Niente affatto d'accordo, invece sul totale asservimento della musica ai particolari più sciocchi, a quei famosi "sincroni secondary" che non solo non servono a nulla ma generano un notevole senso di fastidio nello spettatore, obbligato, nello spazio di 30 secondi, ad ascoltare l'orchestra pronunziare frasi appassionate presto interrotte dal "cattivo" in agguato, al quale segue immediatamente una carrozza che parte, degli starnuti, un padre che piange, una battaglia, un

Marinuzzi here describes the dominant paradigm of film scoring, wherein rapidly contrasting dramatic moments correspond with tight onomatopoeic musical iterations. He expresses a preference for the kind of singular affect that baroque music provides. But tempting as it is to see *The Golden Carriage* as the realisation of Marinuzzi's aesthetic, particularly because of the prescient reference to 'a coach leaving', that would overstate the case. The obvious motivations for using Vivaldi were the coevality of the film's setting and the music's composition, and the common nationality of the theatrical troupe and the composer. That the film is set in South America and the *commedia dell'arte* a metaphorical world away from Vivaldi's milieu matters as little as the actors' contradictory accents (Duncan Lamont's clipped Englishness, Magnani's sing-song Italian – she had learned to speak English for *Vulcano* – and Paul Campbell's American burr). A further motivation is the court setting, which invites scenes of dances and other formal social occasions, with small ensembles occasionally glimpsed through open doors. Renoir offers a further, more subtle rationale:

> Vivaldi's influence obviously had a tremendous influence on the writing of the final shooting script .... It influenced the entire style of the film, a side that isn't drama, that isn't farce, that isn't burlesque. It's a sort of irony that I tried to combine with the light spiritedness one finds, for example, in Goldoni. (Renoir, 1990: 42)

The irony of which Renoir speaks relates to a theme of the film: artifice. It is announced at the beginning of the film with a durationally long, single shot of closed theatre curtains while we hear the strains of Vivaldi's well-known (even at the time) Concerto in E major, first movement, Allegro (RV 293), Spring from the Four Seasons. Camilla later suffers from a sort of Sartrean existential crisis, unsettled by the overlap of playing a role in life and on the stage: 'Where is truth? Where does the theatre end and life begin?' she asks. The answer to those questions is provided in an epilogue, when the curtain closes behind her and she is told by Don Antonio that her lovers are now a part of the audience. For Renoir, then, Vivaldi's music is an expression of contrivance, suffusing the film with appropriate play-fulness.

Individual movements are adopted because of their obvious programmatic appeal. Most come from concertos commonly identified by descriptive titles – L'Inverno, Madrigalesco, Del Gardellino, La Notte, and so on. Nearly all of the

---

panorama, ecc. .... il compositore si è trasformato per necessità in uno di quegli "assaggiatori" di professione, che piluccano un po' di tutto e, in definitiva, non mangiano nulla.' The chapter was entitled 'Aspetti della musica nel film' (pp. 30–48) and the other contributors, all composers, were Nicola Costarelli, Giuseppe Rosati, Vincenzo Tommasini and Antonio Veretti.

concertos existed in editions printed by G. Ricordi and Co., and several of the individual movements were available on LP or 78s (see Table 2).

The opening scene features a bustling Allegro from Vivaldi's Concerto in C major (RV 559), underscoring the gossipy world of the court and its excitable reaction to the coach's arrival. As we cut to the Viceroy having his feet bathed, the third movement of the same composer's Concerto for strings in F major (RV 136), marked Allegro in the score though here performed at a more sedate tempo, introduces a contrasting formal mood. Later, the haunting chromaticism of the first movement of the Sinfonia for strings in B minor, 'Al Santo Sepolcro' (RV 169), evokes the Viceroy's anguish, while more modern comedic connotations of the bassoon are exploited initially to suggest Ramon's unsuitability for Camilla (Concerto for bassoon in E minor, RV 484, first movement) and, later, his and Felipe's immaturity (Concerto for bassoon in B♭ major, RV 501, first movement). Elsewhere, movements from works by Corelli and Martini – the Giga from the former's Violin Sonata Op. 5, No. 9 in A major, the Gavotte from Martini's 1742 Sonate d'intavolatura, originally for organ and harpsichord – provide the instrumental music for the dance scenes.

The various characters of the *commedia dell'arte* are accorded their own themes, played either on solo instrument or by a small ensemble – rustic trumpet, drum, bassoon, piccolo, oboe and percussion. Pantalone plays a theme on the oboe, the Dottore a theme on the bassoon in compound time, the character of Il Capitano a minor-key theme on the trumpet, and the lovers' theme is a lilting 6/8. All of these could either be from popular song – Marinuzzi provided a convincing pastiche for the song sung by Camilla (as Columbine), 'Luna, luna, luna d'argento/Luna piena di sentimento' – though, equally, they could also be forthright, bold statements from the rich source of Vivaldi's instrumental music. Certainly, the Harlequin's theme and the flute's imitation of birdsong that accompanies his and Camilla/Colombine's japing are from the first movement from the Chamber Concerto in D major, 'Del Gardellino' (RV 90). In a 1952 interview in the Italian weekly magazine *Epoca*, Marinuzzi explained that *cannovaci*, essentially templates of sketches and skits which the original performers would then improvise around, included various unattributed melodies that he believed were the work of famous composers.[22] Though he doesn't state it, his assumption may have been that Vivaldi might have been one of them. Either way, the use of such themes in these scenes helps to produce the film's consistent musical palette.

Les Enfants terribles, the sonorisation of *La Passion de Jeanne d'Arc* and *The Golden Coach* all in various ways testify to the influence of the Vivaldi

[22] 'Anna Magnani canterà la tarantella dei maccheroni', *Epoca*, ix(113) (6 December, 1952), 69.

Table 2 List of musical cues and action in *The Golden Coach**

	Timing	Music used (by Vivaldi unless stated)	Action
1.	00:10–02:30	Concerto in E major, Spring (RV 293). First movement: Allegro.	Curtain and credits.
2.	02:34–03:58	Concerto in C (RV 559). First movement: Allegro.	Curtain rises and the coach arrives.
3.	03:59–05:30	Concerto for strings in F major (RV 136). Third movement: Minuet.	Viceroy in his chamber. The stage production.
4.	13:26 – 18:24	Various unidentified pieces, including excerpts from Chamber Concerto in D major, Del Gardellino (RV 90). First movement: Allegro.	Ramon introduces himself to Camilla.
5.	24:20–26.22	Concerto for bassoon in E minor (RV 484). First movement: Allegro.	Backstage and front-of-house views of the performance at the palace.
6.	26:40 – 27:10	Brief burst of (unidentified) solo harpsichord.	The nobility discuss the performance.
7.	27:35–29.00	As 6.	The nobility socialise and dance.
8.	29:13–29:44	Final bars and final cadence of unidentified movement, ending in F major.	The nobility dance while the actors count their takings.
9.	29:46–31:13	As cue 8, followed by Corelli, Violin Sonata Op. 5 No. 9 in A major. Second movement: Giga.	The Viceroy converses with Camilla. The nobility continue their dancing.
10.	31:34–33:16	As cue 3.	

11.	34:04–35:17	Martini, Sonate d'intavolatura for organ and harpsichord (1742). Last movement: Gavotte.	The Viceroy and Camilla continue to converse, observed by others.
12.	35:26–37:15	Concerto for violin in B♭ (RV 380). Second movement: Grave.	The Viceroy and Camilla inspect the coach.
13.	44:43–45:23	Unidentified cue. Fast. Triplet movement.	Camilla and Felipe argue and fight.
14.	51:58–55:05	Concerto for violin in F minor, L'Inverno (RV 297). Second movement: Largo.	Camilla hosts the Viceroy at her home.
15.	55:06–56:20	Concerto for strings in G major, Alla Rustica (RV 151). First movement: Presto.	Camilla arrives to claim her coach.
16.	57:17–59:10	Concerto for strings in G major, Alla Rustica (RV 151). Second movement: Adagio; followed by third movement, Allegro, at 58:12.	The Viceroy meets with the nobles while Camilla and the Marquise observe from separate rooms.
17.	1:06:25–1:09:01	Sinfonia for strings in B minor, Al Santo Sepolcro (RV 169). First movement: Adagio molto.	In front of the noblemen, Camilla accuses the Viceroy of being weak, and leaves.
18.	1:09:12–1:10:04	As 15.	Camilla and the troupe ride off in the coach.
19.	1:11:14–1:13:15	As 17.	The Viceroy laments his plight.
20.	1:13:36–1:17:53	Concerto for bassoon in B♭, La Notte (RV 501). First movement: Largo and Andante molto.	Ramon meets with Camilla. Felipe arrives.
21.	1:18:01–1:20:40	Concerto for two violins and cello in G minor (RV 578). First movement: Allegro.	Camilla greets Felipe.
22.	1:23:12–1:25:12	Concerto for strings and harpsichord in D minor, Madrigalesco (RV 129). First movement: Adagio.	The Viceroy and Camilla converse.

Table 2 (cont.)

	Timing	Music used (by Vivaldi unless stated)	Action
23.	1:27:10–1:27:48	Concerto for strings and harpsichord in D minor, Madrigalesco (RV 129). First movement: Adagio.	The Viceroy and Camilla converse again.
24.	1:28:38–1:29:14/ 1:29:51	Concerto for bassoon in B♭, La Notte (RV 501). First movement: Largo and Andante molto.	The Viceroy leaves. Felipe and Ramon duel and are arrested.
25.	1:33:54–1:35:54	Concerto for violin in C (RV 183). Second movement: Largo.	The Bishop makes his speech, commending Camilla, and instructs everyone on how to behave at the Mass he has organised.
26.	1:36:45–1:37:52	As 25.	Don Alfonso explains to Camilla the relationship between theatre and life.

* All timings from *The Golden Coach* (Jean Renoir, 1952), Digital Classics: 1028DC, DVD.

revival. Though the treatment is different in each, they share a common strategy that has its roots in the compilation-score practices of the silent era, that is, cues are chosen for their suggestive associative affect. Such an approach continues uninterrupted to the present day, with baroque music frequently used anachronistically to evoke an unspecified past or to invite associations of courtliness and religion. But even if the children's social isolation allows them to create a timeless existence, *Les Enfants terribles* shows that a period setting is not a precondition. Instead, a different associative relationship between music and film exists at a cultural level. The recognised aesthete and author of the original novel occupies centre stage, and the film itself is aimed at a culturally literate audience. And that arthouse rationale informs the use of Vivaldi in later films such as *Elvira Madigan* (Bo Widerberg, 1967). Mozart's Piano Concerto No. 21 in C major (K467) is used so obsessively – seven times in the first fourteen minutes – that Mozart's concerto is now commonly identified by the title of the film, and such self-consciously musical orientation encourages and to an extent 'permits' the use of Vivaldi's concertos for violin in E major (L'Amoroso, RV271), G minor (Summer, RV315) and D major (RV230). In more obviously commercial films like *The Bride Wore Black* (1968), François Truffaut's homage to Hitchcock's *Marnie*, with a score by Bernard Herrmann, there is still a certain coyness about using such repertoire non-diegetically, this despite Truffaut's obvious awareness of the use of Vivaldi in *Les Enfants terribles* (see footnote 16 above) and *The Golden Coach*. (Truffaut's admiration for Renoir's *The Golden Carriage* was such that he named his film company after it: Les Films du Carrosse.) The Allegro from Vivaldi's Concerto for mandolin in C major (RV 425) plays over a wistful shot of a white scarf drifting wildly in the wind over Cannes, but its use is prefigured and recapitulated with shots of Julie playing the same music on record players. And something of the same circumspection about baroque music is seen in *The Cowboys* (Mark Rydell, 1972), a John Wayne Western adapted from the novel by William Dale Jennings. One of the boys, Slim Honeycutt (John Carradine) whom Will Anderson (Wayne) hires to help him drive his cattle across country to market, sits with his guitar near the campfire, playing a piece that Will explains 'was written by someone called Veye-valdi' (1.01.15). It is the second movement, Largo, from Vivaldi's Chamber Concerto for lute in D major (RV 93). Having established the identity of the piece, we dissolve to a shot the following morning and the music crosses the fantastical gap to occupy the non-diegetic realm, re-orchestrated by John Williams with a countermelody played on French horn. Baroque music without such careful qualification would not serve as the music track in a mainstream film until the Oscar-winning *Kramer vs. Kramer* (Robert

Benton, 1979), which used the music of Purcell and Vivaldi played on modern instruments.[23] The setting of *Kramer vs. Kramer* is as unambiguously contemporaneous as that of *The Bride Wore Black*, but there is none of that film's hesitation about employing baroque repertoire. The same concerto used in *The Bride Wore Black*, Vivaldi's Concerto for mandolin and strings in C major, is heard over the credits in an arrangement for mandolin and guitar, and next appears diegetically, played by two buskers, to signify the busy sophistication of the Manhattan advertising world in which the main character, Ted, moves. Later the same music accompanies a montage sequence, with motorically insistent rhythms signalling Ted's urgency as he clears away his wife's belongings (23:36–24:05).[24] The use of Purcell's Rondeau Minuet from the incidental music to *The Gordian Knot Untied* (Z597) is deployed to considerably more empathetic ends. As in *Les Enfants terribles*, the slow movement is milked for its affective properties, here arranged for solo strings and continuo, as a self-pitying Ted tidies away his son's toys and tucks him into bed (26:57–28:43). The same music is later arranged for guitar solo with strings (36:47–37:47) when, after a fight with his son, Ted roams the apartment until remorse forces him to look in on him. The Vivaldi trumpet concerto heralds Billy's mastering of a bike and underscores the father's pride (43:21–44:00) while Billy's reunion with his mother (1:08:50–1:09:08) receives a newly composed cue, a unison harpsichord cadenza, the kinetic energy of which matches Billy's joyful running followed by triumphant, trumpet rendition of the theme from Purcell's Rondeau Minuet in the major key.

Ordinary People (Robert Redford, 1980), released a year after *Kramer vs. Kramer*, features what is commonly known as Pachelbel's Canon; this is the first movement of the Canon and Gigue for three violins and basso continuo (PC 358). The music is arranged by Marvin Hamlisch and clearly draws on an earlier and influential 1968 recording by Jean-François Paillard.[25] Coated with a thick patina of tutti strings and distinctive (non-original) pizzicato accompaniment, the same timbral design as the Albinoni Adagio, the recording catapulted the piece into the canon of Popular Baroque Classics. Rather than the famous ground bass, the descending opening theme of the violin part is prominent, played on the piano, frequently in isolation, a hesitant and mournful expression

---

[23] IMDB.com lists a film called *The Money* (Chuck Workman, 1976), the soundtrack of which features four different Vivaldi concertos: www.imdb.com/title/tt0073399/soundtrack?ref_=tt_trv_snd (accessed 19 October 2020). The film was rereleased on VHS as *Atlantic City Jackpot* and marketed around Danny De Vito, who only had three lines in the movie. Unfortunately, I have been unable to get a hold of a copy.

[24] Timings from *Kramer vs. Kramer* (Robert Benton, 1979), Sony Pictures Home Entertainment: CDR10038, DVD.

[25] *Canon in D Major*, Jean-François Paillard Chamber Orchestra, cond. Johann Pachelbel. Musical Heritage Society, MHS 1060 (1968), LP. See also Fink (2011).

of unresolved grief. Until the final credits, *Kramer vs. Kramer* does not acknowledge the score's origins, but in *Ordinary People* the baroque is frequently referenced. The film opens with a piano arrangement of the Canon over shots of nature in autumn. The sound of sopranos singing is heard and we cut to an exterior of a school. Inside, a choir, of which troubled teenager Conrad (Timothy Hutton) is a member, is rehearsing a choral setting of Pachelbel's work. Further references follow. Conrad's soon-to-be girlfriend, after hearing him singing Handel's Hallelujah Chorus behind her in rehearsal, asks him if he likes Vivaldi and Telemann. The later film draws attention to baroque music, making it part of the drama's middle-class setting, whereas in *Kramer vs. Kramer* the repertoire contributes to a more generalised air of control, a displaced expression of the Kramers' constrained dialogue in court and the polite détente that they ultimately reach.

Since 1980, baroque music has been a frequent port of call for musical advisors working in cinema, and unsurprisingly it is Vivaldi's Four Seasons that has been at the top of their list, even providing the title and programmatic structure for the comedy *The Four Seasons* (Alan Alda, 1981). Since the Kaufman 1950 recording (see above section 'The Vivaldi Revival'), more than 200 recordings had been made.[26] A 1969 recording by the Academy of St Martin in the Fields sold over 500,000 copies and earned a gold disc (Argo ZRG 654, LP), by which time the Italian chamber orchestra I Musici had released no fewer than three of their own. Individual movements have also been arranged for, amongst others, voice (The Swingle Singers, *The Joy of Singing*, 1969, Philips PHS 700 004, LP), jazz flute (Moe Koffman, *The Four Seasons*, 1972, GRT – 9230–1022, LP), and koto (The New Koto Ensemble of Japan, *Koto Vivaldi (The Four Seasons)*, 1977, Angel Records – SQ-2–37450, LP). Cinema too has played its part in consolidating Vivaldi's place in the popular consciousness, making him, implausibly, almost a contemporary composer. The abiding aesthetic of the films in which his music is found is broadly integrationist, but there was an alternative approach, one wherein baroque music chafed against narrative cinema's binding of music and image, and which forms the subject of the next section.

3 Bresson, Pasolini and Musical Disconnection

Cinema has always been eager to embrace new musical trends, and the market saturation of newly discovered Italian baroque repertoire against which

---

[26] *The Gramophone*, 'Top 10 Vivaldi Recordings', originally published 11 February 2016, online version www.gramophone.co.uk/features/article/top-10-vivaldi-recordings (accessed 22 October 2020).

Robbins Landon railed in the 1960s pointed the way to a new resource. But at the same time that this new, old repertoire was making its way into narrative cinema, directors outside the mainstream, such as Robert Bresson and Pier Paolo Pasolini, were exploring its formal properties and exploiting them to different, less integrationist ends.

All of the music of Robert Bresson's *Pickpocket* (1959) derives from the first two movements – the Overture and the Passecaille – of Orchestral Suite No. 7 in G minor by the German-born Johann Kaspar Ferdinand Fischer (c.1656–1746). The music originally appeared in his 1695 collection *Le Journal du Printemps*, published in Augsburg and dedicated to Louis William, Margrave of Baden-Baden. However, the film credits the music to the French baroque composer Jean-Baptiste Lully, whom Fischer served as copyist from 1665–71, an error that critics and theorists have perpetuated (Figure 5).

The source of the misattribution appears to be a modern edition prepared by Fernand Oubradous, published as Lully's Suite No. 7 in G minor in 1958 for Éditions Musicales Transatlantiques in Paris and recorded by Oubradous in 1960. Bresson repeated the misidentification in an interview on the radio station France Inter on 9 January 1960, subsequently published as 'Le Masque et la Plume', where he claimed that the music came from a suite by Lully in G minor (Bresson, 2013: 99). Misattribution aside, there is no apparent link between the French or German baroque and the story of a young man, Michel (Martin LaSalle), who learns the craft of pickpocketing, falls in love and is imprisoned. Gone are the obvious connections between the music and the film's subject found in *The Golden Coach* and Lo Duca's version of Dreyer's film – courtliness and period specificity – nor is the music bound tightly to narrative design and exploited for its more obvious associative effects, as is the case in *Les*

Figure 5 From the opening credits of *Pickpocket* (© 1959 Agnès Delahaie Productions Cinématographie / Courtesy of mk2 films)

Enfants terribles. Some critical accounts of *Pickpocket* have discovered a rationale for the music in the equivalence between the dexterity required by Michel's profession and familiar associations of baroque music such as grace, elegance and stateliness.[27] But it is as an articulation of dramatic structure that the baroque music more interestingly and innovatively operates, making a virtue of its overt structures to act as scenic punctuation or to demarcate interscenic segments such as montage sequences and those in which Michel writes in his diary (Jardonnet & Chabrol, 2005: 91–4, 137–40).

Fittingly, the film begins with the overture, including its repeat, consisting of sixteen-bar phrases, beginning and ending on G minor. This same music will be heard later in the film when Michel returns to Paris (62:48) where we once again hear the first sixteen bars of the Overture, creating a rhyme with the beginning of the film.[28] However, the majority of the cues are extracted from the Passecaille. The fifth cue, for example, heard when Michel is making a diary entry (43:10), omits the single bass downbeat and begins on a tutti chord, the same pattern with which the movement begins. This suggests that the music was specially recorded for the film; it is certainly not taken from Oubradous' recording made the following year.[29] The final cue, which begins during the last moments of the final scene and continues over a black screen for nearly a minute beyond (1:10:57–1:12:36), involves considerably more editing: bars 1 to 8, 13 to 16, 57 to 64, 33 to 41 and 89 to 121 (the end of the movement) recapitulate earlier cues: cue 2 (bars 81–105), cue 3 (bars 1 to 8), cue 4 (bars 33 to 41), and so on. These disparate sections, linked by G-minor chords, produce a suite of a suite, with an ostinato, a feature of the passecaille of course, here in the form of a descending, four-bar tetrachord, enabling a modular design of four-bar and eight-bar phrases, thereafter into segments of sixteen and thirty-two bars. Bresson fore-grounds the characteristic symmetry of much baroque instrumental repertoire, a rigid structure that suggests auto-definition, resistant to the undulating contours of narrative or drama, all of which contributes to an impression of music operating independently from the narrative. Bresson is, though, sensitive to

---

[27] 'The stranger silently shows Michel the tricks of the trade in a series of seven shots linked through nearly undetectable dissolves. The fluidity of the effect, as opposed to that of a typical montage, accentuates the **grace, elegance**, and skill associated with a masterly performance, an impression confirmed by the **stately** musical passage from Lully that accompanies it' (Pipolo, 2010: 138); '[Musique] marque, dans un registre **noble** et par là même ironique dans une certain mesure, la détente qui succède à la tension, la joie d'inquiétude' (Sémolué, 1993: 96); 'the **grace** figured by the music' (Reader, 2000: 56). My emphases.

[28] All timings are from *Pickpocket* (Robert Bresson, 1959), Artificial Eye: ART 295 DVD.

[29] Fernand Oubradous, Fernand Oubradous Chamber Orchestra, Robert Gendre (violin); *Leclair Concerto in A minor and Lully Suites Nos. 3 and 7* (Orphée LDO 51.019E, LP). The recording is likewise at modern concert pitch, though noticeably slower than that used in the film.

where such music begins and ends. At a discussion about the film, a member of the public observed how a musical cue begins precisely after Michel has uttered a seemingly banal comment, imparting it with pregnant meaning, and Bresson declared himself touched that his meticulousness had been appreciated (Bresson, 2013: 98). Formal symmetry here is more than a happy convenience; for Bresson, it is an attractive inherent feature of the repertoire. The repertoire is consistent with his view of his films as 'pristine, ascetic objects' (Jones, 1999: 18). His process is one of stripping away frippery, of whittling down dialogue, acting and design to their barest elements, a removal of everything theatrical in all senses of the word. Fischer's music in *Pickpocket* operates as a structural marker, deliberately separated from events by tone and a lack of association. By tracing a line from here to *Mouchette* (Robert Bresson, 1967), which also uses baroque music – Monteverdi's Magnificat from the Vespers of 1610 (SV 206) – one can make a case for baroque music being a feature of authorial style. And because Bresson only uses the music in the opening and closing credits, it is as if this is the last refuge of music in the Bressonian filmic universe before he entirely abandons non-diegetic and extra-diegetic music.

Bresson anticipates a route that baroque repertoire frequently takes after 1960, whereby music is not integrated with drama but essentially punctuative. But in Bresson's case, the disconnection between the chosen music and the fictional world produces a perceptual awareness of an authorial hand, a point made more generally about the use of extant music by Jerrold Levinson, who points to the sense of 'chosenness' that extant music entails (Levinson, 2004: 483). I mentioned this relationship between authorship or narrational presence and music earlier in my account of theorists' response to the use of Vivaldi in *Les Enfants terribles*, and made passing reference to Claudia Gorbman's notion of the auteur *mélomane* (Gorbman, 2007). She expands on the idea of chosenness, pointing out directors in whose films music operates as a marker of authorial style. In the case of baroque music, we can point to Ingmar Bergman's very personal engagement with Bach's music, which more often than not, he uses diegetically (Neumann, 2017). Similarly, Woody Allen, a great admirer of Bergman, uses Bach in some of his films in much the same way (Broman, 2019). And in the specific context of Bach and auteurs *mélomanes*, one must also mention Andrei Tarkovskij. However, none of these directors showed any interest in Bach's contemporaries. These directors focus on a single composer rather than a historically defined repertoire.

The broader issue of the use of any extant music in cinema is a subject that has preoccupied film-music studies. Royal S. Brown argues that any use of extant music evinces a postmodern sensibility (Brown, 1994: 236–63), ineluctably situating music on a parallel plane to the profilmic world. Michel Chion supports this idea in his monograph on *2001: A Space Odyssey* (Stanley Kubrick, 1968) by asserting that such music operates 'outside' of the film (Chion, 2001: 90). Jonathan Godsall goes further, with his acerbic assertion that we hear pre-existing music as music rather than as film music (Godsall, 2018: introduction, unpaginated). What all these arguments presuppose, though, is that extant music is recognised as such, that the listener is familiar with it. As the confusion about the identity of the composer of the music for *Pickpocket* attests, familiarity with Fischer cannot be assumed. And the issue is further complicated by the changing profile of certain pieces of classical music in the years between the release of films and the present day; Kubrick probably did more for Richard Strauss's *Also Sprach Zarathustra* and Wideberg for Mozart's Piano Concerto No. 21 than concert performances or recordings.

All of these issues – the personal relationship between film-maker and (dead) classical composer, the theorisation of that relationship and its implication for the film text, the recognisability of specific repertoire and the spectatorial distraction that such familiarity might provoke – bear on the following discussion of Pier Paolo Pasolini's *Accattone* (1961) and *Mamma Roma* (1962). These were the first two films written and directed by the novelist, poet and outspoken political commentator. Both are set in the Roman *borgate* (slums) of the 1960s and portray the lives of petty criminals, pimps and prostitutes. Consistent with Pasolini's reputation for controversy, *Accattone* in particular was marketed in a sensationalist manner (Schwartz, 2017: 335–6). *Accattone* tells the story of Vittorio (Franco Citti), the *accattone* (scrounger) of the title. He idles his life away in the local bar with his unemployed friends, taking on various challenges, scheming – anything to avoid getting an honest job. He is estranged from his wife and children, and is the pimp of Maddalena. He meets Stella, a virgin whom he seduces and tries to convert to the life of a streetwalker. After trying to turn his life around by getting a paid job, he reverts to crime and, in the course of an attempted robbery, is killed in a random traffic accident. *Mamma Roma* is the story of Ettore, a tough but naïve teenager, who moves from the Friulian region to Rome to live with his mother, Mamma Roma (Anna Magnani). Her ex-husband, Carmine (Franco Citti), blackmails her with the threat of revealing her past as a prostitute to her son, which, ironically, forces her back onto the streets. Ettore befriends local boys and loses his virginity to an older single mother, Bruna, with whom he falls in love. Arrested by the police for petty theft, Ettore dies in hospital. Both films are Christian allegories: Vittorio's life revolves around two Marian figures, Maddalena (Mary Magdalene) and Stella (*Stella Maris*, Star of the of Sea, denoting Mary, mother of Christ) and his final words obliquely reference Christ's crucifixion – 'Ah, I'm fine' ('Ah, io sto bene'), a faint echo of Christ's final words, 'It is finished' (John 19:30) – with Vittorio framed between two thieves; Ettore dies strapped to an iron bed with arms outstretched in a shot modelled on Andrea Mantegna's *Lamentation of Christ* (c. 1480, tempera on canvas, Pinacoteca di Brera, Milan).

One of the most striking features of both films, at first sight and even on repeated viewings, is the counter-intuitive and even bizarre choice of music, evinced by an uncertain and uneven critical response. For *Accattone*, Pasolini uses the music of Bach, and for *Mamma Roma* the music of Vivaldi. While consistent with cultural references such as that to Dante in *Accattone* and to classical painting in *Mamma Roma*, the music produces a considerably more sustained sense of disconnect between high art and the low social status of the characters. It should be said at the outset that Pasolini is not interested in interrogating narrative cinema's sound-image correlations or in textual politics more generally.[30] The neorealist tag sometimes applied to him is misplaced, but he shared with those film-makers the same basic acceptance of dominant conventions of spatial and acoustic organisation (Rhodes, 2004). He himself sought to downplay and even deny the disconnect between music and image in *Accattone*:

> Obviously when I choose music for a film I unfortunately have to take it for granted that the connoisseurs of music will recognize the piece, who plays it, the recording company, and will wonder about my choice, since they won't find it justified. However, the number of people who would feel this way would be quite small and hopefully, after the first moment, even they could overcome this feeling. (Pasolini et al., 1965: 40)

We are close here to what Anahid Kassabian describes as the 'immediate threat of history' (Kassabian, 2001: 3). She draws a distinction between assimilating and affiliating identifications, the former typified by the score composed specifically for a film, one that corrals the spectator into identification with 'socially and historically unfamiliar positions', 'track[ing] perceivers toward a rigid, tightly controlled position that tends to line up comfortably with aspects of dominant ideologies' (Kassabian, 2001: 2 and 141). The affiliating identification, by contrast, allows that the spectator's personal associations with extant music may undermine such determinism. Kassabian does not mean only pop scores; she cites the baroque score of *Dangerous Liaisons*, though she

---

[30] It is interesting to note in passing the distinctly baroque design of cues Godard retained in *Vivre sa vie* (1962). Godard commissioned a score from Michel Legrand but jettisoned all of it, save for a single fragment which he uses almost randomly, or at least without apparent motivation: '[a]s far as the narrative is concerned ... the points where the music plays seem arbitrarily determined' (Brown, 1994: 193). The 12/8 metre, the movement in thirds in the upper line and the simple ostinato bass line are very reminiscent of the accompaniment to recitative 12 of Bach's St Matthew Passion, 'Wiewohl mein Herz in Tränen schwimmt'.

underestimates the contribution of George Fenton (Kassabian, 2001: 69–73. See also Mera, 2001, and Cooke, 2018)). Pasolini, clearly believed that extant music is capable of assimilation, but other theorists would disagree. This is Sergio Miceli talking specifically about Pasolini:

> A universally known piece of music, endowed ... with a solid identity, has an enormous referential power that is closely tied to its natural location and to its traditional use, high or low as it may be. By carrying it abruptly into the cinema, one can cause a ... serious aesthetic imbalance, a disproportion ... between music and image. [Directors] want to carry into their cinematic works music with which they have entertained ... a deep, private and intimate rapport. Theirs is a rapport of mere enjoyment that is dominated by empathy. It therefore is not lucid. (Morricone & Miceli, 2013: 87–8)

The idea of private rapport between director and composer to which Miceli points brings us back to Gorbman's idea of the auteur *mélomane*. Gorbman's concept, though, is a retrospective critical construct, one premised on a body of work and not therefore applicable at the time to Pasolini. While a 'great composer' like Bach could be accommodated by the towering figure of a creative film-maker – a relationship, if not of equals, then based on enduring reputations – the presence of Bach in a film made by a first-time director and set in a squalid milieu is aesthetically imbalanced and disproportionate, to paraphrase Miceli. It even smacks of cultural miscegenation: 'The film has not gained anything from [the music] and [Bach] has definitely lost some majesty' (Pasolini et al., 1965: 39). Bach, it seems, is a problem for *Accattone*. To cite Miceli again, Bach's music is a rich *referential* source, due in no small part to Bach's status as a canonical classical composer of sacred music in particular. Vivaldi, though, carries considerably less cultural baggage, something that Pasolini himself seems ultimately to accept:

> As you can see, I tried to use the same procedure [in *Mamma Roma*] that I had used in *Accattone*; the music in *Mamma Roma* is perhaps less arresting because in a certain sense one could describe it as more logical ... In *Accattone* there was a friction: in fact, between Bach and *Accattone* there is more difference than between Vivaldi and *Mamma Roma*. (Magrelli, 1977: 51)[31]

A consideration of Pasolini's early films thus presents the film-music theorist with a problem. They can, as Mark Brill and others have done, tie *Accattone* to *Il Vangelo secondo Matteo* (*The Gospel According to Matthew*, Pier Paolo

---

[31] 'Come vedi quindi ho cercato di usare lo stesso procedimento impiegato già per *Accattone*; forse la musica in *Mamma Roma* è meno appariscente perché in un certo senso la si potrebbe dire più logica ... In *Accattone* d'era una frizione: infatti tra Bach e *Accattone* c'è più differenza che tra Vivaldi e *Mamma Roma*.'

Pasolini, 1964) because of their common use of Bach's St. Matthew Passion (Brill, 2019). However, Bach's St. Matthew Passion is unambiguously associated with the subject matter in *Il Vangelo* and is the most conventional use of music in a film that elsewhere features Odetta's 'Sometimes I Feel Like a Motherless Child', movements from the Missa Luba, and Blind Willie Johnson's 'Dark Was the Night, Cold Was the Ground'.[32] As Alessandro Cadoni puts it, 'While in the *Gospel* the use of Matthäus Passion appears logical, and the reference to a model on the same subject almost obvious, *Accattone* instead is shaded by a stylistic contamination that results in forceful alienation' (Cadoni, 2004: 21).[33] The gravitational pull of Bach's music, 'widely recognizable [and carrying] a heavy referential power or spiritual connotations (in the sense of being inevitably religious, liturgical or paraliturgical)' (Morricone & Miceli, 2013: 93) is inescapable.

However, the spectre of religiosity that haunts the reception of Pasolini's use of Bach in *Accattone* is exaggerated: half of the four cues were written for secular contexts (slow movements from the Brandenburg Concertos), while the two specifically sacred cues – from the St Matthew Passion and the cantata 'Actus Tragicus' – are devoid of text save for one iteration (as discussed later in this section). Moreover, if the aim was to ally Vittorio's Christological narrative with Christian music, then one might anticipate a similar strategy when it comes to Ettore's equivalent symbolic arc in *Mamma Roma*; instead Pasolini chooses the secular Vivaldi. If anything, rather than synthesising music and narrative symbolism, the abiding image of Bach as a religious composer contributes to the *strangeness* of the reportorial choice. This sense of eccentricity is apparent in accounts that argue for a deliberate policy of contradiction, *Variety*, for

---

[32] Martin Scorsese uses the same chorus, 'Wir setzen uns mit Tränen nieder', in *Casino* (1995). It begins at the choral entry and is synchronised with a shot of an exploding car, which throws its occupant, Sam Rothstein (Robert De Niro), across the screen in an engulfing ball of flame. Garish images of neon signs and hellish conflagration follow in the credit sequence, implying Old Testament vengeance. Images of religiosity abound in the opening ten minutes: a shot of five mobsters at a table recalls Leonardo's *The Last Supper* (a scene described by Scorsese on the DVD commentary as depicting 'pagan gods'); Las Vegas is described in Sam Rothstein's voice-over as a 'paradise on earth [that] washes away your sins'; a helicopter shot of the desert suggests the wilderness where Christ is tempted; and the count room is 'the most sacred ... the holy of holies'. 'I thought it would be more interesting to blast it and have the sense of the music that is sacred music, in a sense. Sacred music, Saint Matthew Passion. Sacred music which is the soundtrack for a story about people who are profane because the idea is that, in Christian thinking, there is no such thing. Every person is worthy of God's love'. Martin Scorsese, commentary on *Casino* DVD 8234271.1–11 / R0. VFB 10475. Music here functions as analogical irony rather than signifying the bestowal of redeeming grace (Vittorio's 'more or less redeemed death') that is promised in *Accattone*. See also Julie Hubbert's argument for musical parallelism in Scorsese's use of music (Hubbert, 2005).

[33] 'Se nel *Vangelo* l'utilizzo della Matthäus Passion appare logico, e quasi scontato il richiamo ad un precedente basato sullo stesso soggetto, in Accattone assume invece le tinte di una contaminazione stilistica dall'impatto fortemente straniante.'

instance: 'A Bach musical adaptation effectively counterpoints action, especially in a fight scene.'[34] Film theorists too have advanced this thesis: 'Bach on the soundtrack in *Accattone* ironically counterpoints the world of pimps, prostitutes, and street-fighters' (Cardullo, 1996: 293).

The use of Bach to Christian ends is further undermined by Pasolini's agnostic conception of the sacred and its encounter with the more specifically Christian connotation of Bach's work.

> In *Accattone* I wanted to represent the degraded and humble human condition of a character that lives in the mud and dust of the Roman *borgate*. I felt, I knew that in this degradation there was something sacred, something religious in an undefined and universal sense of the word, and so I added this adjective, 'sacred', through the music. I said that Accattone's degradation is, yes, degradation, but a degradation somewhat sacred, and I used Bach to explain my intentions to a vast audience. (Pasolini et al., 1965: 40)

The director's personal strain of romantic Marxism is evident here; he celebrates the lives of his characters, discovering in them a nobility and dignity that bourgeois culture otherwise denies. Pasolini's conception of the sacred is complex, and various critics have traced its genealogy and the part it plays in Pasolini's creative output (e.g. Benini, 2015: 18–51). 'The sacred imagined by Pasolini is a spontaneous, "anarchic," noninstitutional sacred, a "forza del Passato" (force of the Past) that is identified with the "senso della terra" (sense of the earth) and the relationship with nature developed by ancient agrarian civilizations' (Benini, 2015: 22). For Pasolini, then, the sacred is a component of an essentialist philosophy. In this light, Ettore's move in *Mamma Roma* from the 'ancient agrarian' Friuli to Rome, the same geographical relocation that Pasolini himself had undertaken, is a nostalgic, autobiographical dramatisation and a personal rediscovery of the sacred and the (technological) profane in the Roman *borgate*. The words 'sacred' and 'religious' when spoken by Pasolini should not, then, be taken as an expression of Christian religion. His understanding is of something more elemental, more pagan even, tied to the earth, and he described the film style of *Accattone* in similar terms (Pasolini, 2015: 210–12) insisting that there is 'nothing more technically sacred than a slow panning shot' (Siti & Zabagli, 2001: 2768).[35]

---

[34] *Variety*, 31 December 1960, by Variety Staff. www.variety.com/1960/film/reviews/accattone-1200420000/ (accessed 6 June 2019). See also Morando Monrandini's review in *Stasera* of 23 November 1961, which talks of 'the slightly cerebral counterpoint of Bach's music' ('il contrappunto un po' cerebrale delle musiche di Bach'). Cited in Parigi, 2008: 226.

[35] 'Non c'è niente di più tecnicamente sacro che una lenta panoramica.' 'Confessione Techniche', originally published in *Uccellacci e Uccellini* (Milan: Garzanti, 1966). There is an obvious resonance here with Luc Moullet's and Godard's reformulation of film form and its relationship to morality. Godard: 'Travelling shots are an issue of morality' ('Les travellings sont affaire de morale') during a round-table discussion of *Hiroshima, mon amour* (Alain Resnais, 1959), and

We thus need to resist the Christian and religious overtones of Pasolini's comments; when we do, we identify a preference for simplicity and clarity of expression in both film and musical form. Bach, through his 'referential power', to use Miceli's phrase, has thrown critics and commentators off the track; Vivaldi, whose music is simpler – 'sentimental, sweet, melodic and thus popular' according to Pasolini – serves the same purpose (Magrelli, 1977: 51). In conclusion, Pasolini was seeking not the referential richness of Bach in *Accattone* but the formal commonality the music shared with Vivaldi. We can thus extend the comments he made about Bach's music in *Accattone* to *Mamma Roma*:

> In [*Mamma Roma*] I wanted to represent the degraded and humble human condition of a character that lives in the mud and dust of the Roman *borgate*. I felt, I knew that in this degradation there was something sacred, something religious in an undefined and universal sense of the word, and so I added this adjective, 'sacred', through the music. I said that [Ettore's and Mamma Roma's] degradation is, yes, degradation, but a degradation somewhat sacred, and I used [Vivaldi] to explain my intentions to a vast audience. (Pasolini et al., 1965: 40 – my interpolations in square parentheses.)

To test this contention, it is necessary to take a more detailed look at the operation of music in both films.

The source for the music in both films is LPs (see table notes for Tables 3 and 4 below). Various edits are made to recorded sound and not at the level of the score itself. The Andante from the Second Brandenburg Concerto, for example, which runs for around four-and-a-half minutes in the original recording, is made to last six minutes and forty-eight seconds at the end *Accattone* (1:48:17 to 1:55:05) by repeating long sections and removing single beats.[36] In *Mamma Roma*, as we will see, Pasolini's approach is somewhat different, revealing a preference for fade-outs rather than editing. Both films adopt motivic programmes, summarised in Tables 3 and 4 below.

Pasolini's musico-motivic design for *Accattone* and some of his explanations do not bear sustained scrutiny. His description of 'mysterious evil' is somewhat opaque, the correlation of musical theme with onscreen relationships is not always consistent and he makes no mention at all of the Adagio from Bach's

---

Luc Moullet's comment about Samuel Fuller's films: 'morality is a question of tracking shots' ('la morale est affaire de travellings', 'morality is a question of tracking shots'). Luc Moullet, 'Sam Fuller: sur les brisées de Marlowe', *Cahiers du cinema*, 93, (March 1959) and Jean Domarchi, Jacques Doniol-Valcroze, Jean-Luc Godard, Pierre Kast, Jacques Rivette and Eric Rohmer, 'Table ronde sur Hiroshima, mon amour d'Alain Resnais', *Cahiers du cinéma*, 97 (July 1959).

36 In scene 76 of *Accattone* there are cuts of two beats: beats 1 and 2 of bar 34; beats 2 and 3 of bar 36; and beats 1 and 2 of bar 37, all of which disrupt the metrical organisation of anacrusis and downbeats. On two occasions men's laughter conceals the cut. All timings are from *Accattone* (Pier Paolo Pasolini, 1961), Eureka Entertainment: EKA 70045, DVD.

Table 3 Pasolini's motivic design for *Accattone*

Pasolini's description (Magrelli, 1977: 50–1) *	Subject/Relationship	Music (all by Bach)
'the "motif of love" that always appeared in the relationships between Accattone and Stella'.	Love motif/ Stella and Vittorio	Brandenburg Concerto no. 2 in F major, (BWV 1047). Second movement: Andante.
'The Passion According to St. Matthew, represented the motif of death and was the dominant motif (a more or less redeemed death)'.	Death motif	St Matthew Passion (BWV 244), final chorus, 'Wir setzen uns mit Tränen nieder'. **
'the Actus Tragicus which was the reason for the "mysterious evil" and I used it when Accattone steals the chain from his son [and] when we see Amore in prison.'	Mysterious Evil	Sonatina from the sacred cantata 'Gottes Zeit ist die allerbeste Zeit' (BWV 106), 'Actus Tragicus'. ***
No reference made by Pasolini.	Maddalena and Vittorio	Brandenburg Concerto No. 1 in F major (BWV 1046). Second movement: Adagio.

* The full quotation from which these references are drawn is: 'I had chosen two or three motifs from Bach: one was the "motif of love" that always appeared in the relationships between Accattone and Stella; another, which was The Passion According to St. Matthew, represented the motif of death and was the dominant motif, (a more or less redeemed death); then there was the Actus Tragicus which was the reason for the "mysterious evil" [and] when we see Amore in prison.' 'Li [in *Accattone*] avevo scelto due o tre motivi da Bach: uno era il "motivo d'amore" che appariva sempre nei rapporti fra Accattone e Stella; un altro, che era La Passione secondo S. Matteo, rappresentava il motivo della morte ed era il motivo dominante (una morte più o meno redenta); poi c'era l'Actus Tragicus che era il motivo del "male misterioso" e l'ho impiegato nel momento in cui Accattone ruba la catenella al figlio, nel momento in cui Amore fa la spia in prigione' (Magrelli, 1977: 50–1).

** The recording of the Passion was made in 1953 and issued by Westminster Records, conducted by Hermann Scherchen with the Vienna State Opera Orchestra and the Vienna Academy Chorus: Westminster WAL 401 (1953), LP.

*** The recording is of the combined forces of the Choir and Baroque Ensemble of the Bach Guild and the Vienna State Opera Orchestra and Choir, conducted by Felix Prohaska, first released as Bach Guild BG-537 (1954), LP, and subsequently reissued as Vanguard SRV-290 (1969), LP, and Bach Guild HM-21 (1972), LP.

Table 4 Pasolini's motivic design for *Mamma Roma*

Pasolini's description (Siti & Zabagli 2001: 2826)	Relationship	Music (all by Vivaldi)
'motif of death'	Mamma Roma/ Ettore	Concerto for viola d'amore and lute in D minor (RV 540). Second movement: Largo.
'motif of destiny'	Mamma Roma/ Carmine	Concerto for flautino in C major (RV 443). Second movement: Largo.
'sensual love'	Ettore/Bruna	Concerto for bassoon in D minor (RV 481). Second movement: Larghetto. *

* The Larghetto from Vivaldi's Concerto for bassoon in D minor (RV 481) is with the Orchestre de la Suisse Romande conducted by Ernest Ansermet, and the soloist is Henri Helaerts. It was first released as SAR643-45 (1952), LP, and the following year as London LS 591 on Decca LX 3100 (1953), LP.

first Brandenburg Concerto. This last cue occurs three times: in two scenes when Vittorio visits Maddalena at his former marital home, where his wife and children still live; and later when Vittorio berates Stella, his new love, whom he accuses of betraying him by sleeping with a client to whom he had introduced her. Magaletta, in a slightly strained argument, suggests that this signals Stella's displacement of Maddalena in Vittorio's affections (Magaletta, 2010: 372). The other slow movement from the Brandenburg Concertos, the Andante from the Second, which Pasolini describes as a love motif and serves clearly enough in that capacity for the most part of the film, works quite differently in the film's final sequence. There it accompanies base comedy – Vittorio and Balilla laughing about Cartagine's smelly feet – and suspense – extreme close-ups of observing eyes. In short, Pasolini's schema is looser than his confident summation suggests. The final chorus of Bach's St. Matthew Passion is similarly multifunctional. Edited to produce a stately instrumental sarabande with the (false) formal coherence of an ABA structure (bars 1–12, 25–36, bars 1–3), it is first heard over the opening credits, where its final cadence synchronises with a quotation from Dante (Figure 6).[37]

---

[37] Those who know the work will undoubtedly anticipate the full chorus entry at bar 13, aurally signalled by the rising quavers of the bass line. Note here Miceli's angry description of 'certain brutal cuts' (Morricone & Miceli, 2013: 88). 'There is also intellectualism, certainly, in *Accattone*: some epigraphic verses of Dante's Purgatory, Bach's music which harshly comments

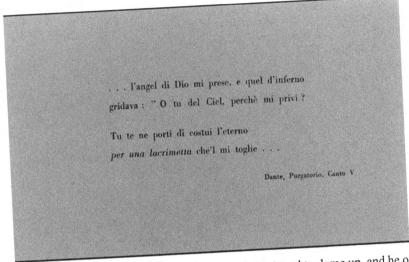

. . . l'angel di Dio mi prese, e quel d'inferno
gridava : " O tu del Ciel, perchè mi privi ?

Tu te ne porti di costui l'eterno
per una lacrimetta che'l mi toglie . . .

Dante, Purgatorio, Canto V

Figure 6 Quote from Dante in *Accattone* * 'God's Angel took me up, and he of hell shouted, "O thou of heaven, why dost thou rob me? Thou bearest away the eternal part of him For one poor little tear, that takes him from me … "'. This translation is available in online subtitle repositories and comes from the Dante Lab website, hosted by Dartmouth College: http://dantelab.dartmouth.edu/ (accessed 6 January 2021). (reproduced by kind permission of Eureka Entertainment) *

The choral contribution of the cue is heard only once in the film ('We sit down in tears / And call to thee in the tomb: / Rest softly, softly rest!' – 'Wir setzen uns mit Tränen nieder / Und rufen dir im Grabe zu: / Ruhe sanfte, sanfte ruh!'), when Vittorio and his brother-in-law fight. There the disjunction between action and music is particularly acute and unsettling. That the music signifies death is an argument easy to make about scene 71, which presages Vittorio's nightmare of his own funeral, but the struggle is less mortal combat than a homoerotic grappling in the dust. Musical signification seems entirely secondary to the synchronisation of physical action and sound, with the first clash of bodies coinciding with the entry of the music.

---

on the rise of vulgarity, the protagonist's dream of death obviously inspired by Bergman (even if the themes of death and the afterlife weigh on this world of the hungry from the outset), the impressive anthology of dialect.' ('C'é anche dell'intellettualismo, sì, in Accattone: alcuni versi del Purgatorio dantesco posti a epigrafe, le musiche di Bach che commentano gravemente le rise de la volgarità, il sogno di morte del protagonista visibilmente ispirato a Bergman (anche se il senso della morte e dell'aldilà pesa dall'inizio su questo mondo di affamati), l'impressionante florilegio dialettale.') Ugo Casiraghi, 'Un lacrimoso melodramma americano e la cruda "opera prima" di Pasolini', *L'Unità*, 1 September 1961. Quoted in Parigi, 2008: 219–20.

This leaves unanswered the question of how the cue is related to death in the scenes when Salvatore and his Neapolitan friends kidnap and beat up Maddalena. Magaletta argues that '[t]he music highlights the sense of death that the Neapolitan represents, his tragedy is equal to that of Accattone' (Magaletta, 2010: 366).[38] In the next scene, though, the music operates empathetically, with the words 'Ruhe sanfte, sanfte ruh' playing twice over three shots (Figures 7a–c): a medium shot of Maddalena lying on the ground, feet towards us; a close-up of her handbag; and a close-up of her shoe, a plangent phrasing that produces a musical gesture of sympathy. Lino Miccichè's recasting of the meaning of Pasolini's motif of death into 'virtual or real violence; and death' is, I think, much more convincing (Miccichè, 1999: 79).[39]

We find similar multifunctionality of musical cues in the case of the Sonatina from Bach's cantata 'Gottes Zeit ist die allerbeste Zeit', which Pasolini argues denotes 'mysterious evil'.[40] The theme is used on three occasions: first, when Vittorio steals his son's necklace; second, when Amore, one of Vittorio's prostitutes, is arrested by the police; and finally, when Amore arrives in prison and meets Maddalena again. In the first case, 'mysterious evil' seems related to a notion of Christian predestination and even original sin. The scene is laden with Christian references: Vittorio's betrayal of his son, the Judas-like kiss that acts as a diversion when he steals the necklace, the resigned acceptance of divine design ('the things I have to do') all recall episodes from the Passion. Again, critics offer different interpretations. Magaletta entirely discounts Pasolini's interpretation and reaches to the cantata's specific history – it was written for a funeral during Bach's years at Mühlhausen (1707–08) (Magaletta, 1997: 366).[41] Miccichè discovers 'the betrayal (of Accattone towards Jaio [his son], of the Sacristan towards Amore, of Accattone towards Maddalena),

---

[38] 'La musica ne rileva il senso di morte che rappresenta il Napoletano, la sua tragedia è parte pari a quella di Accattone.'

[39] 'Tema: la violenza virtuale, o reale; e la morte'.

[40] According to an on-set interview, Elsa Morante was responsible for this cue, which was amongst the earliest of the musical choices. 'The film will have background music by Bach, yet to be chosen, with the exception of the last, which has been fixed as the prelude to the *Actus tragicus*, (also by Bach) following a suggestion by Elsa Morante.' ('Il film si avverà di un sottofondo musicale tratto da Bach e ancora da scegliere, salvo che per il finale, già stabilito con il preludio all'Actus tragicus,(sempre di Bach) consigilato da Elsa Morante.') Cited by De Giusti, 2015: 32.

[41] 'Pasolini uses this sonatina in an appropriate manner whereby Accattone's gesture is that of a man who is waiting to die and who has no future: here is the funereal property of the actus tragicus'. 'Pasolini utilizza questa Sonatina in maniera opportuna in quanto il gesto di Accattone è quello di un uomo che aspetta di morire, che non ha futuro: ecco l'accompagnamento funebre all'actus tragicus.'

Figures 7a–c (a) Maddalena; (b) her handbag; and (c) her shoe (reproduced by kind permission of Eureka Entertainment)

but in an understated and undramatic sense' (Miccichè, 1999: 79). He too, though, is forced to acknowledge that this is at best ambiguous.[42]

Turning to *Mamma Roma*, Pasolini's motivic schema is immediately more convincing. Furthermore, there is a greater uniformity of musical material: all three cues are from slow movements of Vivaldi's solo concertos. The music broadly extends sympathy for the film's sub-proletarian characters: even the emotional blackmailer Carmine is accompanied by a gentle theme played on a delicate wind instrument, the flautino. The bassoon, not an instrument

---

[42] 'Tema: il tradimento (di Accattone verso Jaio, del Sacrestano verso Amore, di Accattone verso Maddalena), ma in sensa non pesante e non dramm'atico.'

traditionally associated with love, illustrates Ettore's puppyish infatuation with Bruna; and the viola d'amore draws on obvious cultural associations to intensify the central relationship of Mamma Roma and Ettore. According to Pasolini's schema, these separate movements relate to destiny, sensual love, and death, and they are unambiguously tied to the film's central relationships. Even when the Concerto for viola d'amore and lute occurs in scene 37, when Ettore learns that his mother is a prostitute, a cue which is otherwise associated with Carmine and Mamma Roma's relationship, it acts as a cruel commentary on the new alignment of a son's feelings, echoing the contempt that Carmine feels for his ex-wife.

As in *Accattone*, music in *Mamma Roma* is often subordinate to film rhythm. In scene 15, for example, music is edited to fit the action, with the entire movement played and then repeated from bar 10 to be faded out at bar 23, to produce a gentle, more general underscore. Overall, though, the later film is more attentive towards music, perhaps a consequence of both experience and a longer period of post-production. Where the earlier film favoured cadential closures, meaning that editing of the original source material is awkward and convoluted, music in *Mamma Roma* is often faded under sirens or shouts, quieter in the mix when there is dialogue and more obviously present when it is not. Furthermore, *Mamma Roma* is considerably more sensitive to local musical structure, with Pasolini cutting shots to musical phrasing, something absent in *Accattone* save for when Maddalena is abandoned by the Neapolitan thugs (see Figures 7a–c). For example, when Ettore is introduced by his friends to Bruna, the opening statement of the Larghetto from the Concerto for bassoon in D minor (RV 481), a mournful unison theme played on strings, solo bassoon and organ continuo (Figure 8c), accompanies an extreme long shot of the six boys (28:43–28:50, Figure 8a).[43] A left-to-right pan across the waste ground coincides with the statement, repeated a fourth higher, suggesting the forced optimism of adolescence (Figure 8b, 28:50–28:57). Just before the phrase ends, we cut to another panning shot of the boys (28:57–29:17, Figure 9a), now right to left, accompanied by a new musical idea (Figure 9b). Two of the boys peel away from the main group (Figure 10) and the camera pans to follow them. The music cadences and we cut back to the remaining four boys. A third musical idea begins, a descending sequential phrase (Figure 11a), accompanying the right-to-left pan-ning shot (29:17–29:37, Figure 11b).

The boys advance on a group of young girls and one of the boys chases after a girl, trying to steal her hat. They disappear behind some ruins and he emerges under a ruined arch, wearing the hat, arriving in place exactly as the music

---

[43] All timings are from *Mamma Roma* (Pier Paolo Pasolini, 1962), Mr Bongo: MRBDVD038, DVD.

Figures 8a–c Sequential phrases aligning with shots; (a) long shot of the boys; (b) pan across waste ground; (c) opening statement of theme (all screen stills from *Mamma Roma*, reproduced by kind permission of Mr Bongo Films)

Figures 9a and 9b (a) Panning shot and (b) new musical idea

cadences (29:37, Figure 12). This moment not only marks the end of the introductory musical material but also brings us exactly to the narrative focus of the scene: Bruna, playing with her baby (Figure 13a). Now we hear the first solo bassoon statement (Figure 13b).

Figure 10 Two boys leave main group

(a)

(b)

Figures 11a and 11b (a) Descending sequential phrase; (b) Four boys peel away from the main group

The sequence shows a greater awareness of small-scale musical form than is apparent anywhere in *Accattone*, and in *Mamma Roma*'s final scenes, where there is extensive cross-cutting between Ettore, who lies dying in hospital, and Mamma Roma at home, that same awareness of musical form is demonstrated at a higher level. The music here is the Largo from Vivaldi's

Figure 12 Cadence and dramatic staging

Figures 13a and 13b (a) Bruna; (b) bassoon solo

Concerto for viola d'amore and lute in D minor (RV 540), and its AABB form is maintained save for occasional small-scale adjustments. The scene begins with Ettore strapped to a bed in the hospital prison with the A section ending as we dissolve to a skylight above his head (1:35:28–1:36:37). The final two bars are repeated, producing an artificial coda which signals a temporal ellipsis (1:36:37–1:36:55), confirmed by an overhead shot of Ettore, now quieted. The camera retreats down his body, framing him from his feet to his head in stark perspective, and the B section begins (1:36:55). Music and editing mark a new episode in which Ettore calls to his mother. As the main refrain starts (end of bar 10, 1:37:17), we cut into a medium close-up; then, as the answering phrase begins (end of bar 12, 1:37:39), we cut to a view from Mamma Roma's apartment. Mamma Roma sits down and pours herself a cup of coffee and the B section is heard as she expresses sorrow for her son (1:38:01). The same musical pattern is now repeated: the main refrain (end of bar 10) aligns with a close-up of Ettore (1:38:21); and the answering phrase (end of bar 12) is synchronised with a shot of Mamma Roma walking along the road (1:38:43). Music plays more than a transitional and structural role; it articulates a telepathy between mother and son.

Mamma Roma does not merely show a greater sensitivity to the use of music in comparison to *Accattone*; it also shows how what might be perceived as the limitations of baroque repertoire – its overt phrasings and foregrounded musical forms – may be exploited without distracting from the otherwise 'invisible' or 'unheard' conventions of narrative film.[44] (In this context, we should acknowledge the contribution of Pasolini's long-term editor, Nino Baragli.) For Pasolini, the achievement of *Mamma Roma* over *Accattone* was the avoidance of the distraction, or 'friction' to use his word, that Bach's music produced. Bach's music was freighted not just with cultural references but also awakened pre-existing spectatorial associations. The solution was to use Vivaldi's concertos in *Mamma Roma* on the grounds that few would be intimately familiar with them. This shows that any experience of disconnection – Brown's parallelism, for example – is contingent on individual response and particularly on familiarity, in which context it is interesting to note that some critics didn't even realise that the music used in *Mamma Roma* was extant.[45] Pasolini had initially believed that prior personal acquaintance with the music or the recording, including his own, could be overwritten, and that new and local metonymic alliances could be forged between music and image that in turn would produce different conditioned responses in the spectator.[46] However, it's possible that he overlooked the crucial role of repetition. That *his* original personal associations

---

[44] Claudia Gorbman traces a similar self-conscious synchronisation of cuts with musical phrasing in *Eyes Wide Shut* (Stanley Kubrick, 1999) and argued that such correspondences function as signifiers of authorial control (Gorbman, 2006: 9).

[45] Leo Pestelli, reviewing the film in *La Stampa*, 1 September 1962, credits all the music to Carlo Rustichelli, the music arranger.

[46] Lauren Anderson questions models of film music that fail to take account of individual response (to popular music) and proposes experimental psychomusicological research and an empirical engagement with audiences in the form of focus groups to address the issue (Anderson, 2016).

with the music had been erased was no guarantee that those of others would be. He had, after all, spent considerable time in the editing room and had been exposed to subsequent screenings, and therefore had accumulated more viewings of his film than the average spectator. By the same token, my repeated viewings of these films for the purposes of analysis have made it more difficult for me to recover the sense of alienation that they induced when I first saw them.

This raises a different, though related issue: the changing profile of appropriated music over time. The place of Bach's music in the classical and popular arenas, in particular the St. Matthew Passion and the Brandenburg concertos, has been fairly consistent over the past seventy-five years, but the same cannot be said of Vivaldi, whose music today is seemingly everywhere – television, films, commercials, hotel lobbies and elevators. Pasolini's profile too has evolved; had he not continued to make films, *Accattone* and *Mamma Roma* would have become merely curios in a poet's life. As it is, his status as a film director is such that Sergio Bassetti, without using the term, can argue that the music in these two films is part of his image as an auteur *mélomane* (Bassetti, 1998). Such a view, as I have argued and as the criticism's levelled against Pasolini about the use of Bach attest, was not possible at the time of the film's release.

But what is the process by which musical familiarity is overwritten by new meaning? To answer that we need to take account of film form, musical form and their interactions; musical history and musical reception; and the processes of reprogramming of musical material in film. Such a model was outlined in succinct if embryonic form by Claudia Gorbman, who anticipated this critical requirement with a simple distinction between cultural musical codes and cinematic musical codes. The model has recently been revised and reformulated by David Neumeyer, who recasts Gorbman's cultural musical codes and cinematic musical codes as topic and trope (Neumeyer, 2015: 183–265, Figure 14).

The topic (cultural musical code) is stable and familiar, 'a conventional musical sign with an unusually clear signification' (Buhler, 2014: 208), examples of which might be a trumpet fanfare to signify the martial or the ceremonial, or a swooning solo violin to signify love.[47] The trope (cinematic musical code) is less stable and more dependent on (re-)iteration within a single film or franchise. Obvious examples would be motifs or themes related to characters, such as the Bond theme, the Darth Vader theme and so on. Disquiet about the use of baroque music, and Bach in particular, arises because

---

[47] Neumeyer and Buhler coined the term 'style topic' for their film-music primer. See Buhler, Neumeyer & Deemer (2010: 195–215).

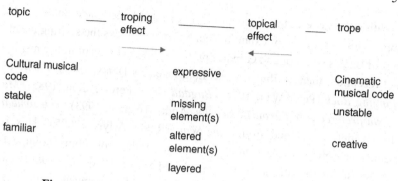

Figure 14 David Neumeyer schema (Neumeyer, 2015: 185)

the associative potential of familiar music is so great that it inhibits or retards the troping effect. From that premise follows an argument whereby any recoding, however localised or repetitious, cannot convincingly negate foreknowledge and personal association.

That Bach is a special case is a common refrain in this article; Bach is a composer who, while clearly of the baroque, also and by virtue of his status as one of the Great Composers, somehow exceeds his era. As noted earlier, Bergman uses Bach mainly diegetically, associating performance and the music itself with the film's characters and milieu (Neumeyer, 2015: 190–234 and 235–265; and Neumann, 2017). Such diegetic placement of music is potentially a more convincing invitation to the spectator to abandon their personal associations than the use of the same music non-diegetically. After all, the diegetic world, if not entirely co-extensive with the world that the spectator inhabits (science fiction and fantasy are obvious exceptions), is premised on shared assumptions and acknowledgements of human behaviour, experience and culture. The identification of the composer of diegetic music is commonplace, often acknowledged by the film's characters, while non-diegetic music is covert, the identification of the composer limited to the extra-diegetic space of the credits. When a character sits down to play the piano, for example, it is more likely than not that it will be an extant composition, unless it is marked as being composed by a character (Michael's performance of 'Were You Smiling At Me' in *Les Enfants terribles*, for example). In turn, this explains why films such as *2001: A Space Odyssey* are viewed as exceptions to the more general rule that non-diegetic music is specially composed rather than drawn from extant sources.[48]

---

[48] I have made this point in a slightly different form elsewhere, contrasting the diegetic use of 'real' medieval music in *Joan of Arc* (Victor Fleming, 1948) with the considerably later non-diegetic accommodation of equivalent music nearly fifty years later in Jacques Rivette's two-part biopic, *Jeanne la Pucelle I – Les batailles* (1994) and *Jeanne la Pucelle II – Les prisons* (1994) (Greig, 2019, 252–3).

With a keen eye to the distinction between the diegetic and non-diegetic implications of the use of extant music, Neumeyer tracks the shifting meanings of Bach's C-major and G-major preludes, first in terms of music history and reception, then in films such as *Lola* (Jacques Demy, 1961), *Picnic at Hanging Rock* (Peter Weir, 1975), *Bagdad Café* (Percy Adlon, 1985), *Ma saison préférée* (*My Favourite Season*, André Téchiné, 1993), *Entrapment* (Jon Amiel, 1999) and *Following Sean* (Ralph Arlyck, 2005). This is Neumeyer's most worked-through account of the trope/topic argument, a synthesis of the film semiotics developed in the 1970s and 1980s and Robert Hatten's and Raymond Monelle's work on music semiotics. Neumeyer's analyses also highlight the consequences of performance tempo, drawing a parallel between faster speeds and neutrality on the one hand, and slower speeds and emotion on the other: 'The unflagging étude-like manner of many recorded performances of the C Major Prelude minimizes expressive qualities of the music and can lead to its use as neutral underscore or as narratively indifferent end-credits music' (Neumeyer, 2015: 201). For the 'étude-like manner' read the 'sewing-machine' style of performance. At the other end of the scale, as it were, slow movements and slow tempi serve as expressive vehicles of grief and more general sadness. The Pachelbel canon in *Ordinary People* is a case in point, a piece that owes its popularity to twentieth-century invention. And the spirit of pastiche or reinvention applies to two other baroque 'classics' with similarly counterfeit, or allegedly counterfeit, status: the Bach Toccata and Fugue in D minor and the Albinoni/Giazotto Adagio in G minor. As noted, the former's original and very specific horror-film association of the 1930s has seen it reused in similar contexts many times. The Albinoni/Giazotto has a similar history, used mainly empathetically in *The Trial* (Orson Welles, 1962), *Gallipoli* (Peter Weir, 1981), *Rollerball* (Norman Jewison, 1975), *Flashdance* (Adrian Lyne, 1983), parodied in *Inbetweeners 2* (Damon Beasley and Iain Morris, 2014), and also used in *Manchester by the Sea* (Kenneth Lonergan, 2016) and most recently in *Dogs Don't Wear Pants* (Jukka-Pekka Valkeapää, 2019). The repeated use of these cues in cinematic contexts perfectly demonstrates Neumeyer's argument about tropes. 'A troping effect', he explains, 'is laid on a topic when it is treated in an expressive rather than neutral fashion, an effect that is *cumulative*' (Neumeyer, 2015: 185, my emphasis). Historical associations have been overlaid by cinematic associations to the point where Albinoni ceases to be a Venetian composer, and Pachelbel is merely the identifying name by which a single piece is known: 'Gorbman's cinematic musical code [has] harden[ed] into the cultural musical code' (Neumeyer, 2015: 186).

4 Authenticity and Historically Informed Performance

The majority of baroque music used in cinema discussed thus far derives from recordings made before 1960, all of which were played on modern instruments in equal temperament and at modern pitch, that is A=440 Hz. And of those recordings, a surprising number were conducted by Jean-François Paillard and Herbert Von Karajan, both of whom favoured somewhat soupy orchestrations and languorous tempi for slow movements. While similar interpretations continue to the present day, since the 1950s smaller forces, original instruments, gut strings, alternative tunings, a pitch standard of A=415 Hz and research-based instrumental techniques have carved out a place for themselves in the concert and recording worlds. The issue of authenticity was a hot topic for musicological debate in the 1970s and 1980s and became a badge performers were happy to wear to signal their modern(ist) commitment to historical reconstruction. At the same time, the musicological community, perhaps conscious of its role as a superego, began to question its own essentially corrective stance, noting that emerging performance styles owed much to modernist trends and therefore reflected modern preoccupations. The publication in 1988 of a set of essays devoted to the subject, followed in 1995 by books by Richard Taruskin and Peter Kivy, ensured that authenticity would thereafter be used more hesitantly by performers and record labels, and be marked in academic circles by the use of scare quotes (Kenyon, 1988; Taruskin, 1995; Kivy, 1995). In its place came the more carefully qualified ideal of historically informed practice, a term whose acronym, fortuitously – and perhaps even aspirationally – made its proponents sound, well, hip.

Jean-Marie Straub and Danièle Huillet's *The Chronicle of Anna Magdalena Bach* (*Chronik der Anna Magdalena Bach*, 1968) is an intriguing and early incursion of HIP into cinema. To the early-music aficionado, it is an historical document in its own right, featuring the contributions of Gustav Leonhardt, who plays the harpsichord and also 'plays' the role of Bach. He is joined by the Concentus Musicus (Vienna) directed by Nikolaus Harnoncourt, the concert group of the Schola Cantorum Basiliensis, and the Hanover Boys' Choir, all performers committed to historical performance research and practice (Rubinoff, 2011). As in many of Straub and Huillet's other films, *Chronicle*'s hallmark is a dispassionate, objectivist attitude to drama, with characters delivering their lines almost uninflected, in Bressonian manner. Informed ultimately by Bertolt Brecht's theories of dramaturgy, editing is minimal and direct sound is used throughout. There is no non-diegetic music. Ostensibly a biopic, the film's subject, J. S. Bach, is very much off-centre, literally so in some of the framings, a very different conception to that of *The Great Mr*

Handel or other similarly conventional scenarios wherein psychology explains musical creation. Bach is not the hero and is less a genius than a labourer, figured as the nexus of economic and ideological forces – religion, the family, patronage. Anna Magdalena, Bach's second wife, 'chronicles' a period of his life in voice-over, with no embellishment, dramatic illustration, dialogue or, most importantly, narrative causality. In colloquial terms, nothing happens. Consequently, there is a focus on the here-and-now of the various musical performances. These lengthy sequences are shot often from the side rather than frontally: this is musical performance observed rather than presented to an implied or actual audience, with precious little cutting within scenes, the very antithesis of the heavily edited recordings that digital technology has encouraged. The recreation of historical performance is not, though, the film's purpose, nor authenticity its universal aim. That much is evident in the eschewal of dramatic modes of verisimilitude; we do not see 'Bach' age, something one might otherwise expect of a film that pays such close attention to period detail in wigs, clothing, instruments, musical techniques, and even spectacles (Rubinoff, 2011: 7). The actuality of music and performance in real time is matched by the focus on the actuality of documents, presented as if in a slide show with masked corners – autograph manuscripts, letters, documents, contracts and so on. Straub and Huillet's adoption of HIP, a regulative ideology, would seem to be potentially at odds with a film that the directors describe as Marxist, but it is a logical extension of their materialist philosophy; musical performance is a consequence of historical determinism rather than an act of individual creation (Straub, 1969).

No such ideological considerations inform *Tous les matins du monde* (Alain Corneau, 1991). This biopic of a lesser-known French baroque composer, Sainte-Colombe, and his pupil Marin Marais is another film notable for its performance research and musico-historical exactitude. Unlike *Chronicle*, *Tous les matins* was avowedly mainstream and had considerable success, winning seven César Awards and the 1993 Golden Globe Award for Best Foreign Language Film. It was thus a more significant film for the advancement and demystification of HIP, with esoteric baroque repertoire and its mainly diegetic performance set within a conventional narrative. Music here serves as an expression of individual psychology: Sainte-Colombe's playing summons his dead wife; Marais is the young apprentice striving to gain the hand of Sainte-Colombe's daughter by becoming a composer/performer, like her father. The viola da gamba player of the soundtrack, Jordi Savall, was the musical director, and also coached the actors in playing the viol, bringing a further imprimatur of authenticity to the proceedings, but his contribution, unlike Leonhardt's and Harnoncourt's in *Chronicle*, remains unseen. The actors mime to his playing and approximate it, whereas the musicians in *Chronicle* are seen working, their reality as performers visible beneath wigs and period costume.

Given the nature of these films, it might appear that the only way HIP could make inroads into cinema was diegetically, with performers the subject of films, as if this strange new way of playing needed to be justified in historical terms. This would echo the hesitant incursion of baroque music in films like *The Bride Wore Black* and *The Cowboys*, where baroque music is initially grounded diegetically before occupying an unambiguously non-diegetic zone. Similar anxiety about baroque music meant that even an auteur *mélomane* like Stanley Kubrick felt the need to commission the film-music composer Leonard Rosenman to arrange movements from concertos by Bach and Vivaldi for *Barry Lyndon* (1975) rather than using extant recordings. And it is notable that Kubrick's distrust of the affective power of baroque repertoire was such that he felt no music from that era could adequately serve as a love theme (Baxter, 1997: 293).

One can posit a different fault line between mainstream and HIP in narrative cinema by comparing two cinematic adaptations of Pierre Choderlos de Laclos' *Les Liaisons Dangereuses*. *Valmont* (Miloš Forman, 1989) manifests the earlier mainstream performance approach – modern instruments, modern pitch – with the Academy of St Martin in the Fields conducted by Sir Neville Marriner, some five years after their success with *Amadeus* (Miloš Forman, 1984), which performs music by mainly French baroque composers (Lully, Couperin, Charpentier, Rameau), though also plenty of (anachronistic) Mozart and Haydn. *Dangerous Liaisons* (Stephen Frears, 1988) skilfully concealed the joins between Handel and George Fenton's stylistically convincing compositions, performed on both original and modern instruments and at baroque pitch (Mera, 2001), a hybridised blend of ancient and modern amplified by reference not just to Handel but also to Bernard Herrmann's score for *North by Northwest* (Cooke, 2018).[49] Two films by Lars von Trier, *Dogville* (2003) and *Manderlay* (2005), take a different approach (Greig, 2020a). These were part of a planned trilogy entitled the Land of Opportunities, a sly commentary on America, the third of which, *Wasington* [*sic*], was never made. The first two are notable for their obvious theatrical design, with simple sets, narrator, chapter headings and minimal props. While these features, together with disruptions of classical modes of editing and overt political themes, suggest Brecht's epic theatre, the approach is more fabular than interventionist. In part, this is a consequence of the director's renowned self-publicisation and deliberate sh(l)ock tactics, though, to be fair, von Trier didn't make Brechtian claims for the films, merely

---

[49] Mera and Cooke report Fenton's instruction to the copyist to account for both modern pitch and baroque pitch given the hybrid nature of his orchestra (Mera, 2001: 13; and Cooke, 2018: 41)

saying that the idea of *Dogville* sprang from a fragmentary thought about the playwright.[50] The more obvious precedent is the eighteenth-century novel and, significantly, von Trier cites *Barry Lyndon* as inspiration. The music for both films is arranged by Joachim Holbeck, von Trier's musical director since *Medea* (Lars von Trier, 1988), and it is performed on period instruments and at baroque pitch by the English Concert Orchestra (presumably, moonlighting players of the English Concert). In the main, the music is allied to narrative events and is taken from the slow movements of baroque concertos or instrumental section of choral works by Vivaldi, Handel, Pergolesi and Albinoni. In *Manderlay*, the rising chromatic instrumental lines of the fourth movement of Vivaldi's solo psalm setting, Nisi Dominus (RV 608, c.1716), for example, provide an air of ominous anticipation of the coming storm. Elsewhere, major keys and busy counterpoint lend an air of optimistic industry to a montage of work activities. Mainly, though, the music's overt cultural and historical properties keep the drama at a distance. The music is filleted so that cues begin with firmly stated themes and end on clear cadences, distilling the formality of eighteenth-century musical design into musical vignettes that occupy the same peri-diegetic space as John Hurt's gravelly narrator. Such episodic punctuation recalls Bresson's approach in *Pickpocket*, though the generally restrained HIP style contributes to a mode of detached irony. However, HIP is fairly incidental; it is not difficult to imagine performances on modern instruments and at modern pitch that could have accommodated a demand for expressive disengagement. While HIP has been characterised as objectivist, more inclined than the mainstream towards crisp articulation, metronomic rigidity and cool disengagement, that is a generalised and inaccurate view. As Fabian and Butt have pointed out, many HIP exponents have advanced opposite values, crafting passionate and metrically fluid interpretations (Butt, 2002: 32; Fabian, 2003: 97–133). That von Trier opted for HIP is, I suspect, less due to ideology than performance trends and the availability of specialist musicians in the marketplace.

With a diegetic orientation of musical performance, the Purcell biopic *England, My England* (Tony Palmer, 1995) benefits from the period performances of John Eliot Gardiner and the English Baroque Soloists, but the success of the HIP movement is such that one is now almost as likely to encounter a recording on original instruments as a mainstream recording in a commercial film. In short, HIP is now to cinema just another musical resource, which does not mean that certain films do not manifest a clear preference for HIP

---

[50] Von Trier cites the German playwright as the 'secondhand inspiration' deriving from an Oedipal attachment – his mother was keen on Brecht; more specifically, that it derived from Pirate Jenny's song from Brecht's 1928 play, *The Threepenny Opera*, composed by Kurt Weill (Björkman, 2003: 245). For Brechtian readings, see Jovanovic (2017), and Koutsourakis (2015).

recordings. That is certainly true in the case of *The Favourite* (Yorgos Lanthimos, 2018), a dark comedy, which favours orchestras who proudly wear HIP on their sleeves. Recordings of baroque music by the English Concert, Ars Antigua and the English Baroque Soloists are part of an eclectic palette that embraces Messaien, Schumann, contemporary classical music and a song by Elton John. For all the implied respect accorded to Purcell, Vivaldi and Handel in the adherence to HIP, Lanthimos's approach to baroque music is cavalier if inventive. Indeed, one wonders what the commentator who condemned Pasolini for making Bach less majestic might have said about a scene where a naked man in a pink wig is pelted with oranges for sport to the strains of Bach's Fantasia in C minor (BWV 562) (1:12:00–1:13:41).[51] The film begins with a shot of Queen Anne being divested of her ceremonial robe, accompanied by the opening four bars of the first movement, Largo, of Handel's Concerto Grosso in B♭, Op. 6, No. 7 (HWV 325), a sequential passage that comes to rest on the dominant (01:01–01:27). Rather than following on in time, the music is halted to allow the Queen (Olivia Colman) and Lady Marlborough (Rachel Weisz) to converse. The title of the film is now spelled out and the next two phrases of four and six beats respectively are separated and interspersed with dialogue as Lady Marlborough is blindfolded and led by the Queen down a secret passage to receive a gift, an architectural model, presumably of Blenheim Palace (01:59 – 02:05 and 02:09–02:18). Again, dialogue halts the flow of the music before returning after a new title, 'I: THIS MUD STINKS'. We cut to Abigail (Emma Stone), who is travelling in a carriage to the Queen's palace (02:52–03:16). Similar musical segmentation applies later in the film, again to accommodate dialogue. As the Queen is wheeled into her bedroom, we hear the first four bars of the Adagio from Purcell's Trumpet Sonata in D major (Z850). The music now stops and a line of dialogue is uttered by the controlling Lady Marlborough: 'You will pronounce the tax in Parliament: I will set the date.' The music returns with the next four bars, closing the scene (35:44–36:21). Much as the fish-eye lenses, used at various moments throughout the film, distort straight horizontal and vertical lines, so filmic logic unsettles the formal symmetry of the baroque repertoire.

5 The Neo-baroque, the New Baroque and Minimalism

As noted, the music track for *The Favourite* is eclectic and by no means limited to music of the period in which the film is set. During a sequence in which Abigail finds her way into the Queen's bedroom, the Queen rails against

---

[51] All timings are from *The Favourite* (Yorgos Lanthimos, 2018), 20th Century Fox Home Entertainment: F1-83308-DVD-SV.1, DVD.

Parliament, and Lady Marlborough plots, we hear the regular, repeated sound of a G played on a viola with a scraping bow (56:49–1:02:04). After a little more than a minute, it is joined by what sounds like a plucked cello (it is actually prepared piano), playing the same G in alternation with the viola. With no prior knowledge, one might imagine that this cue was the creation of a music consultant or even sound engineer, so basic is its design. It is, in fact, the opening of *Didascalies*, a 2004 composition for viola, piano, memorised sound and computer by Luc Ferrari, a member of Pierre Schaeffer's Groupe de Musique Concrète and co-founder with him of the Groupe de Recherches Musicales. The composition consists of several musical formulae of which we hear numbers one and two (which carry a marking of obsessional – *obsédent*) and, with its (somewhat gnomic) instructions, not dissimilar in design to the minimalist composer Terry Riley's *In C*. Ferrari admired Riley's composition and was similarly impressed with Steve Reich's early work, and though not generally seen as a minimalist, in a 1998 interview he talked of developing his own conception of minimalism (Robindoré & Ferrari, 1998: 13). The stripping back of music to its essentials and the concomitant focus on texture and timbre shares with the HIP movement an interest in restoration like that of paintings which, in the popular imagination at least, means the removal of a thick, discoloured accretion of lacquer to reveal the clean lines beneath. A similar fascination with 'pure' textures and sound is found in popular oddities like Wendy (née Walter) Carlos's *Switched-on Bach*, echoes of which were heard in film in the 1970s. Released on Columbia Records in 1968, *Switched-on Bach* was a collection of Bach's music – two-part inventions, Preludes and Fugues, better-known works ('Jesu, Joy of Man's Desiring', 'Air on a G String' and 'Wachet auf') and the complete Third Brandenburg Concerto in G major – played on the Moog synthesiser. The album topped the Billboard classical chart from 1969 to 1972 and reached number 10 in the Billboard 200. It led indirectly to Carlos's work for Kubrick in *A Clockwork Orange* (1971), with the music of Purcell providing a British orientation that balances the central character's preoccupation with Beethoven ('lovely, lovely Ludwig van'). The Moog synthesiser's expressive limitations epitomised inhuman reproduction and the mathematical precision for which baroque music stood, and though there were no connections between Carlos and minimalist composers, all shared an interest in clinical timbres. It was the minimalist composers' interest in such textures, but also in mathematicity and musical systems, that prompted the 'pervasive and variegated critical trope' of the New Baroque (Fink, 2005: 170). This 'sociojournalistic trope' (Fink, 2005: 12) was responsible for perpetuating caricatures of both minimalist and baroque music, as seen in the following:

Bach and Handel excepted, most baroque music is, like Minimalism, music of pattern. Your typical Corelli, Vivaldi, Locatelli, or Geminiani concerto grosso is virtually devoid of personality or imagination. It moves in a purely sequential pattern, its harmonies circumscribed largely to tonic, dominant, and subdominant chords … Its excuse for being was that it wrapped the listener in innocuous sound, the busy patterns moving up and down without ever really saying anything. (Schonberg, 1985)

The New Baroque pointed to a commonality of musical features, particularly small-scale structures like arpeggiation and the sequence. It posited 'a great unison sounding through the history of music', that could be traced from 'the long series of arpeggios through the cycle of fifths' in Bach's Cello Suites to Philip Glass's 'ecstatic arpeggios' (Sheffer, 1997: iv). Minimalist composers had distilled the overt stylistics features of baroque music and made them into what Steve Reich described in a manifesto as 'perceptible processes' (Reich, 2002). Musical style and form became signifiers of the repertoire itself, touching on the properties of abstractness and mathematicity that are frequently cited in the context of baroque repertoire, and recapitulating an image of the earlier repertoire as self-involved.[52] Furthermore, as Fink points out, minimalism updated the same socially based mode of repeated listening which, according to Langdon's sketch, the Vivaldi revival precipitated in Manhattan soirees, appropriately enough, given New York's reputation as one of the centres of minimalism (Fink, 2005: 169–207).

More concretely, minimalist composers' appropriations of baroque models by modernist composers have warranted the term neo-baroque. The word is more likely to be encountered in discussions of architecture and pipe organs than in a music context, where it is subsumed under the umbrella term neoclasicism, in turn inherited from the visual arts (Messing, 1988: 80–5). Neo-classicism was first used in music criticism in 1923 with reference to Igor Stravinsky's Octet of that year and his 1920 ballet suite, *Pulcinella*, based on what was at the time taken to be the work of the early-eighteenth-century composer Giovanni Battista Pergolesi (Messing, 1988: 87–8).

The most prominent proponent of the neo-baroque in cinema was Michael Nyman, who hailed not from New York but from Britain. Nyman had links with both baroque music and with minimalism. He had pursued, though ultimately abandoned, a PhD on seventeenth-century 'systems music' at King's College, London, supervised by Thurston Dart, and also produced editions of Purcell's

---

[52] 'Regardless of which term was employed by the architects of the avant-garde during the decade between *Le sacre du printemps* and the Octet, the definitions for *nouveau classicisme* and *néoclassicisme* invariably contained a common vocabulary: abstract, absolute, architectural, pure, concise, direct, and objective' (Messing, 1988: 88).

catches and Handel's Concerti Grossi Op. 6 (Siôn, 2007: 23 & 25). As a critic, composer and advocate of minimalism, he had interviewed Reich in 1970, and staged a concert of Reich's ensemble at London's ICA the following year, reviewed minimalist recordings and concerts in his role as a journalist, and written a book, *Experimental Music: Cage and Beyond* in 1974. He established a working relationship with Peter Greenaway in the 1970s and shared with him a preference for baroque models:

> Michael Nyman and I were very excited by the music coming out of New York in the 50s and 60s – people like Steve Reich and Philip Glass – and the combination of minimalist music and baroque music which often uses the same language. They use repetitive cycles, variation on a very strict theme, a great sense again of the list and the grid in a musical way. (McBride, 1992: 57)

The upshot was the use of specific composers and baroque forms: the score for Greenaway's *1–100* (1978) was a stylistic importation of Vivaldi; his *A Walk Through H* (1978) expressed a fascination with baroque devices like the sequence; and Monteverdi and Biber were the sources for *Making a Splash* (1984) and *A Zed and Two Noughts* (1985) respectively. However, it was *The Draughtsman's Contract* (Peter Greenaway, 1982) that really announced the Greenaway/Nyman collaboration to the world. The film's convoluted and ultimately unresolved murder-mystery plot, in which a rich female owner of a country house, Mrs Virginia Herbert (Janet Suzman), contracts an arrogant artist, Mr Neville (Anthony Higgins), to produce twelve paintings in exchange for sexual favours, finds its visual analogue in the precision of the drawings, the careful framings and compositions of the film camera and the stark horizontals and verticals of Mr Neville's perspective grid. Similarly, the broad theme of artifice and device (in the sense of a ploy), and the ornate yet proper language, find an acoustic analogue in Nyman's neo-baroque score.

The debt to Purcell in *The Draughtsman's Contract* was explicit. The film is set in 1694, a year before Purcell's death, and, according to Nyman's liner notes to the original soundtrack, its models are recognisably 'reconstruct[ed], renovat[ed], renarrat[ed], refocus[ed], revitaliz[ed] rearrang[ed] or just plain rewritt[en]'. The honking reeds hark back to Nyman's more medievalist experiments with rebec, shawms and sackbuts for the Campiello Band, which he assembled for the National Theatre's production of Goldoni's *Il Campiello*, and the result is a score that is recognisable and recognisably distorted Purcell. The film opens to the sound of countertenor accompanied by harpsichord, performing 'At Last the Glittering Queen of Night' from Purcell's Ode on the Assembly of the Nobility and Gentry of the City and County of York (Z333). The original lyrics by Tom D'Urfey are altered to fit the ensuing drama, making reference to gardens, but it is an otherwise fairly faithful rendition in terms of performance practice. As the scene is set, we also hear the same countertenor voice singing the song, 'She Loves and She Confesses Too' (Z413). Both pieces function mainly diegetically, though there is no visual confirmation of this. From here, we shift to Nyman's re-compositions and 'The Disposition of the Linen' (13.31–14.23), the model for which is 'She Loves and She Confesses Too'.[53] Bass strings produce chugging quavers, over which violins present the opening bars of the tune. 'An Eye for Optical Theory' follows a similar approach with the Ground in C minor (ZD221, actually attributed to William Croft) though more obviously rewritten (16.33–18:01). The ground itself is played on farting bassoons, while strings beat out repeated quavers to foreground rhythmic organisation, thereafter joined by stiff woodwind which carries the main theme. In both cases, rather like the Paillard treatment of the Pachelbel Canon, further counter-themes are added and the main theme disappears. The Chaconne from Suite No. 2 in G minor (ZT680) can easily be perceived in the dirge-like 'A Watery Death', with bassoons bleating out its main theme, initially accompanied by metallic chords and joined later by repeated quaver iterations from woodwind and strings (1:37:19–1:39:23). Cues like this and 'Bravura in the Face of Grief' (53.12–55:00 and 1:32:43–1:33:42) draw on the affective properties of the original model, here the plaint 'O, Let Me Weep' from Act 5 of *The Fairy Queen*, to illustrate Mr Neville's undoing. For the main part, the finer points of baroque performance practice such as mordents, trills and 'spread' chords are jettisoned in the service of metronomic tempi, and the music functions as 'works imperfectly remembered and reproduced' (Fink, 2004: 554).

Nyman's American forebears, Reich, Riley and Glass, all worked with experimental film-makers in the 1960s and early 1970s, but it was only Glass who would work as a composer for mainstream film (Doran Eaton, 2013: 183–8). His less-intellectual though similarly knowing appropriation of baroque design is apparent in his score for *Koyaanisqatsi* (Godfrey Reggio, 1982). Glass frequently uses ground bass, often played by that quintessentially baroque instrument, the organ, over which he places repeated arpeggiated sequences, recalling the design of many fast movements of Italian baroque concertos where a superstructure of scalar or arpeggiated semiquaver movement is laid over a rigid rhythmic bass/base. The insistence on rhythmic pattern – its perceptible process – is further underlined by a predilection for synchronising cuts with

---

[53] All timings from *The Draughtsman's Contract* (Peter Greenaway, 1982), British Film Institute: BFIVD563, DVD.

musical cells. Glass's film scores were not always neo-baroque. The two films that followed *Koyaanisqatsi*, and with it formed a trilogy, were less obviously modelled on baroque principles. *Powaqqatsi* (Godfrey Reggio, 1988) featured Latin rhythms and Arabic scales, and the cello of Yo-Yo Ma in *Naqoyqatsi* (Godfrey Reggio, 2002) provided rhythmically free solos and a much more romantic feel. Glass's later score for the horror film *Candyman* (Bernard Rose, 1992), however, resembles that for *Koyaanisqatsi* in several ways: the scoring for organ and (often wordless) voices, repeated musical cells, the use of Alberti bass, and arpeggiation in the upper parts. And, indeed, the commonality of the musical and filmic design is emphasised by the use of high overhead shots of urban settings, which recall the similarly shot, man-made and natural large-scale grid patterns of *Koyaanisqatsi*. As *Candyman*'s more obvious horror elements are revealed, the organ and choral voices, both common tropes in horror-film music, are repurposed.

To film-makers like Reggio, Greenaway and Rose, the arrival of the neo-baroque was clearly welcome. This form of minimalist music could evoke the past and connote the traditional roles that baroque music furnished – stateliness, formality, religiosity – yet its modern idiom and connections to Manhattan evoked a contemporary urban environment. Its musical style provided metrical order, rhythmic regularity and familiar, repetitive harmonic patterns. Gone was the need for editing of extant baroque music; new music with the same properties could be composed to fit screen time. Vivaldi was available for hire.

6 Final Thoughts

This necessarily selective survey demonstrates that baroque music in the concert hall, on recordings and in the cinema manifests a broad array of styles, and that its performance, arrangement and re-imag(in)ing embrace traditions that postdate the period in which the repertoire was composed. The neo-baroque in particular highlights the stylistic features of baroque repertoire that potentially act as constraints in a cinematic context, constraints that are found at the level of rhythm and metre. In turn, this sheds some light on why such repertoire remains an exception to the dominant paradigms of film music, such as the late-romantic tradition of the Hollywood Golden Era. Individual movements of baroque concertos, sinfonias and suites are defined by metre, be it a dance form – the 3/4 of the minuet or sarabande, the 12/8 of the siciliano – or basic tempi indications, be they 4/4, 3/4, or any other. Metrical contrast is discovered *between* movements, not within them. Furthermore, baroque instrumental music, more than other repertoire, favours symmetries and has a modular design. Phrases and musical ideas, which, as the analysis of *Mamma Roma* shows, are often in two- and four-bar units, are subject to repetition. Variety within a movement is restricted. Charles Rosen puts it thus: 'When a rhythm has been established, it is generally continued relentlessly until the end ... Once the piece is underway an impression of *perpetuum mobile* is not uncommon' (Rosen, 1976: 61). Furthermore, the metaphor of the sewing machine, condescending as it is, recognises that a straightjacketed adherence to mathematical metricality is to a degree determined by musical design and the demands of ensemble. Crotchets, quavers and semiquavers interlock, necessarily so if ensemble is to be convincing. Those playing the larger units must follow the smallest articulated units, and fast movements in particular are played at such a speed that small-scale temporal variation is simply not possible. While such variation is certainly achievable in slow movements, in fast movements rhythmic regularity and repeated rhythmic repetition is, to an extent, dictated by musical style.

Compare this to the practice of conventional narrative film music, where rhythmic flexibility was key. Max Steiner, amongst many others, would begin by laying out a grid of regularised beats – the click track – onto which a more irregular metre, answerable to the musical and dramatic contours, could be applied.[54] Such practice is evident in film-scoring manuals of later years: 'Never, and that means <u>NEVER</u>, squeeze your music ... Try to find a shift in the bar line to pick up the time your need. Try to change 4/4 bar to 3/4, or two 3/4 bars to 5/4 rather than rush to make a timing' (Hagen, 1971: 74). In the modern era, metrical variation still applies, with SMPTE timecode and notational software enabling the temporal flexibility that conductors used to achieve in the studio era, resulting in tempo markings calculated to tenths of a second. The contradictory requirements of baroque music's regular metre and film music's irregular barring is clearly demonstrated in David Raksin's Bach-inspired score for *The Redeemer* (Joseph Breen, 1965). 'The melodies are all varied as required within individual sequences', Raksin writes, 'with meter signatures of 3/4, 2/4, 5/4 and a few others.'[55] Raksin bowed to the dominant film-music system that applied at the time to override baroque music's inflexibility.

It is, I believe, in such properties of metrical rigidity that we find one explanation for the common use of baroque repertoire in cinema as

---

[54] See Jacobs (2015), 221–3.

[55] David Raksin, quoted in Prendergast (1977), 151. *The Redeemer* (aka *Los misterios del rosario*) was produced by the Family Theatre, the film production unit of the Catholic Church, and originally made for television as fifteen half-hour segments. Further details are provided in ibid., 148–50.

a distancing device – as episodic punctuation and as peri-diegetic commentary. Furthermore, the demand for rhythmical fluidity that drama makes on film explains why it is the later, more rhythmically pliant repertoire that has become the dominant paradigm. None of which means that baroque music will not continue to be used in cinema.

Bibliography

Abbado, Michelangelo (1942). *Antonio Vivaldi*. Turin: Arione.

Abbado, Michelangelo (1979). Antonio Vivaldi nel nostro secolo con particolare riferimento alle sue opere strumentali. *Nuova Rivista musicale Italiana*, 13, 79–112.

Adams, Stephen J. (1975). Pound, Olga Rudge, and the 'Risveglio Vivaldiano'. *Paideuma*, 4(1), 111–18.

Agawu, Kofi (1991). *Playing with Signs: A Semiotic Interpretation of Classical Music*. Princeton: Princeton University Press. DOI: https://doi.org/10.1515/9781400861835

Allanbrook, Wye Jamison (2002). Theorizing the Comic Surface. In Andreas Giger and Thomas J. Mathiesen (eds.), *Music in the Mirror: Reflections on the History of Music Theory and Literature for the Twenty-First Century*. Lincoln, NE: University of Nebraska Press.

Altman, Rick (2004). *Silent Film Sound*. New York: Columbia University Press.

Anderson, Gillian B. (1987). The Presentation of Silent Films, or, Music as Anaesthesia. *Journal of Musicology*, 5(2), 257–95. DOI: https://doi.org/10.2307/763853

Anderson, Laura (2013). The Poetry of Sound: Jean Cocteau, Film and Early Sound Design (PhD dissertation, Royal Holloway College, London).

Anderson, Laura (2021). Music as a Sonic Enabler: Jean-Pierre Melville's Film Adaptation of Jean Cocteau's *Les Enfants terribles*. In M. Baumgartner and E. Boczkowska (eds.), *Music and Auteur Filmmakers in European Art House Cinema of the 1950s to the 1980s: Individuality and Identity*. Abingdon: Routledge.

Anderson, Lauren (2016). Beyond Figures of the Audience. *Music, Sound, and the Moving Image*, 10(1), 25–51. DOI: https://doi.org/10.3828/msmi.2016.2

Auerbach, Erich (1953). *Mimesis: The Representation of Reality in Western Literature*, trans. Willard R. Trask. Princeton: Princeton University Press.

Bassetti, Sergio (1998). Letteratura musicale tra passione e ideologia nel cinema di Pier Paolo Pasolini. In Sergio Miceli (ed.), *Norme con ironie: scritti per I settant'anni di Ennio Morricone*. Milan: Suvini Zerboni, pp. 29–75.

Baxter, John (1997). *Stanley Kubrick: A Biography*. London: Harper Collins.

Benini, Stefania (2015). *Pasolini: The Sacred Flesh*. Toronto: University of Toronto Press. DOI: https://doi.org/10.3138/9781442669871

Bergstrom, Janet (1996). Jean Renoir's Return to France. *Poetics Today*, 17(3), 453–89. DOI: https://doi.org/10.2307/1773418

Bergstrom, Janet (2009). Genealogy of *The Golden Coach*. *Film History: An International Journal*, **21**(3), 276–94. DOI: https://doi.org/10.2979/fil .2009.21.3.276

Björkman, Stig (ed.) (2003). *Trier on von Trier*, trans. Neil Smith. London: Faber and Faber. DOI: https://doi.org/10.5040/9780571344925

Bordwell, David (1973). *Filmguide to La Passion de Jeanne d'Arc*. Bloomington: Indiana University Press.

Bresson, Robert (2013). *Bresson par Bresson: Entretiens (1943–1983)*, ed. Mylène Bresson. Paris: Flammarion. DOI: https://doi.org/10.14375/np .9782081298583

Brill, Mark (2019). The Consecration of the Marginalized: Pasolini's Use of J. S. Bach in *Accattone* (1961) and *Il Vangelo Secondo Matteo* (1964). *Bach*, **50**(2), 220–53. DOI: https://doi.org/10.22513/bach.50.2.0220

Broman, Per F. (2019). Another Woody: J. S. Bach in Dixieland, *Bach*, **50**(2), 254–74. DOI: https://doi.org/10.22513/bach.50.2.0254

Brown, Royal S. (1994). *Undertones and Overtones: Reading Film Music*. Berkeley: University of California Press. DOI: https://doi.org/10.1525 /9780520914773

Buhler, James (2014). Ontological, Formal, and Critical Theories of Film Music and Sound. In David Neumeyer (ed.), *The Oxford Handbook of Film Music Studies*, Oxford: Oxford University Press, pp. 187–226. DOI: https://doi.org /10.1093/oxfordhb/9780195328493.013.005

Buhler, James, Neumeyer, David and Deemer, Rob (2010). *Hearing the Movies: Music and Sound in Film History Hearing the Movies: Music and Sound in Film History*. New York: Oxford University Press.

Bukofzer, Manfred (1947). *Music in the Baroque Era: from Monteverdi to Bach*. New York: Norton.

Burch, Noël (1952). *Les Enfants terribles*. *Institut des hautes études cinématographiques: Fiche filmographique*, **94**, 1–10.

Butt, John (2002). *Playing with History: The Historical Approach to Musical Performance*. Cambridge: Cambridge University Press. DOI: https://doi.org /10.1017/cbo9780511613555

Cadoni, Alessandro (2004). Cinema e musica 'classica': il caso di Bach nei film di Pasolini. https://users.unimi.it/gpiana/dm9/cadoni/cadoni.html, unpaginated (accessed 5 October 2018). Published as La musica di Bach nel cinema di Pier Paolo Pasolini: *Accattone* e *Il Vangelo secondo Matteo*. *Quaderni Casarsesi*, **9**, 21–8.

Cardullo, Bert (1996). Smoke and Tears. *The Hudson Review*, **49**, 286–93. DOI: https://doi.org/10.2307/3852464

Chiarini, Luigi and Masetti, Enzo (ed.) (1950). *La musica nel film*. Rome: Bianco e Nero.

Chion, Michel (2001). *Kubrick's Cinema Odyssey*, trans. Claudia Gorbman. London: British Film Institute.

Cohen, Harriet (1969). *A Bundle of Time: The Memoirs of Harriet Cohen*. London: Faber & Faber.

Comisso, Irene (2012). Theory and Practice in Erdmann/Becce/Brav's *Allgemeines Handbuch der Film-Musik* (1927). *Journal of Film Music* 5(1–2), 93–100. DOI: https://doi.org/10.1558/jfm.v5i1-2.93

Cooke, Mervyn (2008). *A History of Film Music*. Cambridge: Cambridge University Press. DOI: https://doi.org/10.1017/cbo9780511814341

Cooke, Mervyn (2018). Baroque à la Hitchcock: the Music of *Dangerous Liaisons*. In James Cook, Alexander Kolassa and Adam Whittaker (eds.), *Recomposing the Past: Representations of Early Music on Stage and Screen*. Abingdon: Routledge, pp. 32–50.

Cooke, Mervyn (ed.) (2010). *The Hollywood Film Reader*. Oxford: Oxford University Press.

Corbella, Maurizio (2015). Gino Marinuzzi Jr: Electronics and Early Multimedia Mentality in Italy. *Musica/Tecnologia*, **8–9**, 95–133.

Cormack, Mike (2006). The Pleasures of Ambiguity: Using Classical Music in Film. In Phil Powrie and Robynn Stilwell (eds.), *Changing Tunes: The Use of Pre-existing Music in Film*. London: Routledge, pp. 19–30. DOI: https://doi.org/10.4324/9781315095882-2

De Giusti, Luciano (2015). Preludio della Passione secondo Pasolini. In Luciano De Giusti and Roberto Chiesi (eds.), *Accattone: l'esordio di Pier Paolo Pasolini raccontato dai documenti*. Bologna: Edizioni Cineteca di Bologna, pp. 9–46.

Doering, James M. (2019). Status, Standards, and Stereotypes: J. S. Bach's Presence in the Silent Era. *Bach*, **50**(20), 5–31, DOI: https://doi.org/10.22513/bach.50.1.0005

Doran Eaton, Rebecca M. (2013). Minimalist and Postminimalist Music in Multimedia: From the Avant-Garde to the Blockbuster Film. In Keith Potter, Kyle Gann and Pwyll ap Siôn (eds.), *The Ashgate Research Companion to Minimalist and Postminimalist Music*. Aldershot: Ashgate, pp. 181–200. DOI: https://doi.org/10.4324/9781315613260-20

Downes, Olin (1950). Vivaldi Revival. In *The New York Times*, 30 April.

Dreyfus, Lawrence (1983). Early Music Defended Against Its Devotees: A Theory of Historical Performance in the Twentieth Century. *The Musical Quarterly*, **69**(3), 297–322. DOI: https://doi.org/10.1093/mq/lxix.3.297

Duflot, Jean (ed.) (1970). *Entretiens avec Pier Paolo Pasolini*. Paris: Belfond.

Erdmann, Hans, Becce, Giuseppe and Brav, Ludwig (1927). *Allgemeines Handbuch der Film-Musik.* Leipzig: Schlesinger'sche Buch.

Fabian, Dorottya (2003). *Bach Performance Practice 1945–1975: A Comprehensive Review of Sound Recordings and Literature.* Aldershot: Ashgate. DOI: https://doi.org/10.4324/9781315096698

Fabian, Dorottya (2015). *A Musicology of Performance: Theory and Method Based on Bach's Solos for Violin.* Cambridge: Open Book Publishers. DOI: https://doi.org/10.11647/obp.0064

Ferro, N. (1977) *Mamma Roma* ovvero, dalla responsabilità individuale alla responsabilità collettiva: conversazione con Pier Paolo Pasolini. In Enrico Magrelli (ed.), *Con Pier Paolo Pasolini.* Rome: Bulzoni, pp. 43–62 (originally *Filmcritica*, 125 (1962)).

Fertonani, Cesare (1989). Edizioni e revisioni vivaldiane in Italia nella prima metà del Novecento (1919–1943). *Chigiana*, **41**(21), 235–66.

Nicolodi, Fiamma (1980). Vivaldi nell'attività di Alfredo Casella organizzatoe e interprete. In Francesco Degrada (ed.), *Vivaldi veneziano europeo*, Florence: Olschki, pp. 303–32.

Fink, Robert (2004). (Post-)minimalisms 1970–2000: The Search for a New Mainstream. In N. Cook and A. Pople (eds.), *The Cambridge History of Twentieth-Century Music*, Cambridge: Cambridge University Press, pp. 539–56. DOI: https://doi.org/10.1017/chol9780521662567.022

Fink, Robert (2005). *Repeating Ourselves: American Minimal Music as Cultural Practice.* Berkeley: University of California Press.

Fink, Robert (2011). Prisoners of Pachelbel: An Essay in Post-Canonic Musicology. *Hamburger Jahrbuch für Musikwissenschaft*, **27**, 89–104.

Fuchs, Maria (2014). 'The Hermeneutic Framing of Film Illustration Practice': The *Allgemeines Handbuch der Film-Musik* in the Context of Historico-Musicological Traditions. In Claus Tieber and Anna Windisch (eds.), *The Sounds of Silent Films: New Perspectives on History, Theory and Practice.* Basingstoke: Palgrave Macmillan, pp. 156–71. DOI: https://doi.org/10.1057/9781137410726_10

Giazotto, Remo (1945). *Tomaso Albinoni: "musico di violino dilettante Veneto" (1671–1750).* Milan: Fratelli Bocea.

Giegling, Franz (1949). *Giuseppe Torelli: ein Beitrag zur Entwicklungsgeschichte des italienischen Konzerts.* Kassel: Bärenreiter.

Godsall, Jonathan (2018). *Reeled In: Pre-existing Music in Narrative Film.* Abingdon: Routledge. DOI: https://doi.org/10.4324/9781315266558

Gorbman, Claudia (2006). Ears Wide Open: Kubrick's Music. In Phil Powrie and Robynn Stilwell (eds.), *Changing Tunes: The Use of Pre-existing Music in Film*. London: Routledge, pp. 3–18. DOI: https://doi.org/10.4324/9781315095882-1

Gorbman, Claudia (2007). Auteur Music. In Daniel Goldmark, Lawrence Kramer and Richard Leppert (eds.), *Beyond the Soundtrack: Representing Music in Cinema*, Berkeley: University of California Press, pp.149–62.

Greene, Naomi (1990). *Pier Paolo Pasolini: Cinema as Heresy.* Princeton: Princeton University Press. DOI: https://doi.org/10.1515/9781400887064

Greig, Donald (2019). Re-sounding Carl Theodor Dreyer's *La Passion de Jeanne d'Arc*. In Stephen C. Meyer and Kirsten Yri (eds.), *The Oxford Handbook to Medievalism and Music*. Oxford: Oxford University Press, pp. 247–66. DOI: https://doi.org/10.1093/oxfordhb/9780190658441.013.17

Greig, Donald (2020a). Lars von Trier, Brecht and the Baroque Gesture. In Carol Vernallis, Holly Rogers, and Lisa Perrott (eds.), *Transmedia Directors: Music/Sound/Image*. New York: Bloomsbury, pp. 389–96. DOI: https://doi.org/10.5040/9781501339295.0041

Greig, Donald (2020b). Lo Duca and Dreyer: Baroque Music, Extant Recordings and Aleatoric Synchrony. *Music and the Moving Image*, **13**(2), 25–61. DOI: https://doi.org/10.5406/musimoviimag.13.2.0025

Greig, Donald (2021). 'Somewhat of an Affectation': Bach and Vivaldi in the Early Films of Pier Paolo Pasolini. *Music and Letters* (in press).

Hagen, Earle (1971). *Scoring for Films: A Complete Text*. New York: Criterion Music.

Haskell, Harry (1988). *The Early Music Revival: A History.* London: Thames and Hudson.

Hubbert, Julie (2005). Bach and the Rolling Stones: Scorsese and the Postmodern Soundtrack in Casino. In Andreas Dorschel (ed.), *Tonspuren: Musik und Film, Musik im Film Studien zur Wertungsforchung*. Vienna: Universal Editions, pp. 43–69.

Jacobs, Lea (2015). *Film Rhythm after Sound: Technology, Music, and Performance*. Berkeley: California University Press.

Jardonnet, Evelyne, and Chabrol, Marguerite (2005). *Pickpocket de Robert Bresson*. Paris: Atlande.

Jones, Kent (1999). *L'Argent*. London: British Film Institute.

Jovanovic, Nenad (2017). *Brechtian Cinemas: Montage and Theatricality in Jean-Marie Straub and Danièle Huillet, Peter Watkins, and Lars von Trier.* Albany: State University of New York Press.

Kassabian, Anahid (2001). *Hearing Film: Tracking Identifications in Contemporary Hollywood Film Music*. New York & London: Routledge.

Kenyon, Nicholas (ed.) (1988). *Authenticity and Early Music*. Oxford: Oxford University Press.

Kivy, Peter (1995). *Authenticities: Philosophical Reflections on Musical Performance*, Ithaca: Cornell University Press.

Koutsourakis, Angelos (2015). *Politics as Form in Lars Von Trier: A Post-Brechtian Reading*. London: Bloomsbury Academic.

Lang, Edith and West, George (1920). *Musical Accompaniment of Moving Pictures: A Practical Manual for Pianists and Organists and an Exposition of the Principles Underlying the Musical Interpretation of Moving Pictures*. Boston, MA: Boston Music.

Leech-Wilkinson, Daniel (2002). *The Modern Invention of Medieval Music*. Cambridge: Cambridge University Press.

Lerner, Neil (2009). The Strange Case of Rouben Mamoulian's Sound Stew: The Uncanny Soundtrack in Dr. Jekyll and Mr. Hyde (1931). In Neil Lerner (ed.), *Music in the Horror Film*. New York: Routledge, pp. 55–79. DOI: https://doi.org/10.4324/9780203860311

Levinson, Jerrold (2004). Film Music and Narrative Agency. In Leo Braudy and Marshall Cohen (eds.), *Film Theory and Criticism: Introductory Readings, Sixth Edition*, Oxford: Oxford University Press, pp. 143–83. DOI: https://doi.org/10.1093/acprof:oso/9780199206179.003.0010

Lo Duca (1949). Triologia mistica di Dreyer. *Cinema* 14, 422–5.

Lo Duca (1952). Trilogie mystique de Dreyer. *Cahiers du Cinéma* 9, 60–3.

Lowe, Melanie (2002). Claiming Amadeus: Classical Feedback in American Media. *American Music*, **20**(1), 102–19. DOI: https://doi.org/10.2307/3052244

Lugert, Wulf Dieter and Schütz, Volker (1998). Adagio à la Albinoni. *Praxis des Musikunterrichts*, **53**, 13–22.

Magaletta, Giuseppe (1997). *La musica nell'opera letteraria e cinematografica di Pier Paolo Pasolini*. Urbino: Quattro Venti.

Magaletta, Giuseppe (2010). *Pier Paolo Pasolini: Le opere, la musica, la cultura*, Volume 2, *Cinema*. Foggia: Galiani.

Magrelli, Enrico (1977). *Con Pier Paolo Pasolini*. Rome: Bulzoni.

Mann, Alfred, and Knapp, J. Merrill (1969). The Present State of Handel Research. *Acta Musicologica*, **41**(1/2), 4–26

Marchesini, Alberto (1994). *Citazioni pittoriche nel cinema di Pasolini (da Accattone al Decameron)*. Florence: La Nuova Italia.

Masetti, Enzo (ed.) (1950). *La musica nel film*. Rome: Bianco e Nero.

McBride, Stephanie (1992). G Is for Greenaway. *Circa*, **62**, 52–7. DOI: https://doi.org/10.2307/25557721

Mera, Miguel (2001). Representing the Baroque: The Portrayal of Historical Period in Film Music. *The Consort: Journal of the Dolmetsch Foundation*, **57**, 3–21.

Messing, Scott (1988). *Neoclassicism in Music: From the Genesis of the Concept through the Schoenberg/Stravinsky Polemic*. Ann Arbor: University of Michigan Press.

Miccichè, Lino (1999). *Pasolini nella città del cinema*, Venice: Marsilio.

Mirka, Danuta (2014). Introduction to Topic Theory. In Danuta Mirka (ed.), *The Oxford Handbook of Topic Theory*. Oxford: Oxford Handbooks Online. DOI: https://doi.org/10.1093/oxfordhb/9780199841578.013.002

Morricone Ennio, and Miceli, Sergio (2013). *Composing for the Cinema: The Theory and Praxis of Music in Film*, trans. Gillian B. Anderson. Lanham, MD: Scarecrow Press.

Neumann, Anyssa (2017). Sound, Act, Presence: Pre-existing Music in the Films of Ingmar Bergman (PhD diss., King's College, London).

Neumeyer, David (2015). *Meaning and Interpretation of Music in Cinema*. Bloomington: Indiana University Press.

Nogueira, Rui (ed.) (1971). *Melville on Melville*, trans. Tom Milne. London: Secker & Warburg.

Parigi, Stefania (2008). *Accattone*. Turin: Lindau.

Pasolini, Pier Paolo (1966). *Uccellacci e Uccellini*. Milan: Garzanti.

Pasolini, Pier Paolo (1988). Comments on Free Indirect Discourse. In *Heretical Empiricism*, trans. Ben Lawton and Louise K. Barnett. Bloomington: Indiana University Press, pp. 79–101.

Pasolini, Pier Paolo (2015). Una sacralità tecnica. In Luciano De Giusti and Roberto Chiesi (eds.), *Accattone: l'esordio di Pier Paolo Pasolini raccontato dai documenti*. Bologna: Edizioni Cineteca di Bologna, pp. 210–12. (Originally from interview with Gideon Bachmann, 20 July 1966, Fonda Gideon Bachmann – Cinemazero, Pordenone.)

Pasolini, Pier Paolo, with Fioravanti, Leonardo, and Zulficar, Omar, et al. (1965). Pier Paolo Pasolini: An Epical-Religious View of the World. *Film Quarterly*, 18(4), 31–45. DOI: https://doi.org/10.1525/fq.1965.18.4.04a00050

Paul, Catherine E. (2016). *Fascist Directive: Ezra Pound and Italian Cultural Nationalism*. Clemson: Clemson University Press. DOI: https://doi.org/10.5949/liverpool/9781942954057.001.0001

Pincherle, Marc (1948). *Antonio Vivaldi et la musique instrumentale*, 2 vols (Paris: Floury).

Pincherle, Marc (1954). *Corelli et son temps*. Paris: Editions Le Bon Plaisir.

Pincherle, Marc (1956). *Corelli: His Life, His Work*, trans. Hubert E. M. Russell. New York: W.W. Norton.

Pipolo, Tony (2010). *Robert Bresson: A Passion for Film*. New York: Oxford University Press.

Pound, Ezra (1977). *Ezra Pound and Music: The Complete Criticism*, ed. Murray R. Schafer. New York: New Directions.

Prendergast, Roy M. (1977). *Film Music: A Neglected Art*. New York: Norton.

Rapée, Ernö (1924). *Motion Picture Moods for Pianists and Organists*. New York: Schirmer.

Rapée, Ernö (1925). *Encyclopaedia of Music for Pictures*. New York: Belmont (reprinted, New York: Arno Press, 1970).

Reader, Keith (2000). *Robert Bresson*. Manchester: Manchester University Press.

Reich, Steve (2002). Music as a Gradual Process. In Paul Hillier (ed.), *Writings about Music, 1965–2000*. Oxford and New York: Oxford University Press, pp. 9–11. DOI: https://doi.org/10.1093/acprof:oso/9780195151152.003.0004

Renoir, Jean (1990). *Renoir on Renoir: Interviews, Essays, and Remarks*, trans. Carol Volk. Cambridge: Cambridge University Press.

Rhodes, John David (2004). 'Scandalous Desecration': *Accattone* Against the Neorealist City. *Framework*, **45**, 7–33.

Rinaldi, Mario (1943). *Antonio Vivaldi*. Milan: Istituto Alta Cultura.

Rinaldi, Mario (1978). Vita, morte e risurrezione di Antonio Vivaldi. *Studi musicali*, **7**, 189–213.

Rinaldi, Mario (1980). Itinerario della rivolutazione Vivaldiana: Vivaldi veneziano europeo. In Francesco Degrada (ed.), *Vivaldi veneziano europeo*. Florence: Olschki, pp. 289–302.

Robbins Landon, H. C. (1961). A Pox on Manfredini. *High Fidelity*, **11**(6).

Robindoré, B., and Ferrari, L. (1998). Luc Ferrari: Interview with an Intimate Iconoclast. *Computer Music Journal*, **22**(3), 8–16. DOI: https://doi.org/10.2307/3681154

Rosen, Charles (1976). *The Classical Style: Haydn, Mozart, Beethoven*. Revised edition. New York: Viking Press.

Rubinoff, Kailan R. (2011). Authenticity as a Political Act: Straub-Huillet's *Chronicle of Anna Magdalena Bach* and the Post-War Bach Revival. *Music and Politics*, **5**(1), 1–24.

Rühlmann, J. (1867). Antonio Vivaldi und sein Einfluss auf Johann Sebastian Bach. *Neue Zeitschrift für Musik*, 63.

Schonberg, Harold C. (1985). Plumbing the Shallows of Minimalism. *The New York Times*, 21 February, Section C, p. 18.

Schwartz, Barth David (2017). *Pasolini Requiem*, 2nd ed. Chicago: University of Chicago Press. DOI: https://doi.org/10.7208/chicago/9780226335162.001.0001

Sémolué, Jean (1993). *Bresson, ou L'acte pure des métamorphoses*. Paris: Flammarion.

Sheffer, Jonathan (1997). Foreword. In Claudia Swan (ed.), *Perceptible Process: Minimalism and the Baroque*. New York: Eos. pp. i–v.

Siôn, Pwyll ap (2007). *The Music of Michael Nyman: Texts, Contexts, and Intertexts*. Aldershot: Ashgate.

Siti, Walter and Zabagli, Franco (eds.) (2001). *Pasolini per il Cinema*, Vol. 2. Milan: Mondadori.

Stack, Oswald (1969). *Pasolini on Pasolini*. Bloomington: Indiana University Press.

Steimatsky, Noa (1998). Pasolini on *Terra Sancta*: Towards a Theology of Film. *The Yale Journal of Criticism*, **11**(1), 239–258. DOI: https://doi.org/10.1353 /yale.1998.0024

Straub, Jean-Marie (1969). Post-scriptum de J.-M. Straub. *Cahiers du cinéma* **212**: 10.

Talbot, Michael (1988). *Antonio Vivaldi: A Guide to Research*. New York and London, Garland Publishing, Inc.

Talbot, Michael (1994). *Tomaso Albinoni: The Venetian Composer and his World*. Oxford: Clarendon Press.

Taruskin, Richard (1988). The Pastness of the Present and the Presence of the Past. In Nicholas Kenyon (ed.), *Authenticity and Early Music*. Oxford: Oxford University Press, pp. 137–210.

Taruskin, Richard (1995). *Text and Act: Essays on Music and Performance*. Oxford: Oxford University Press.

Tootell, George (1927). *How to Play the Cinema Organ*. London: Paxman.

Turk, Edward Baron (1980). The Film Adaptation of Cocteau's *Les Enfants terribles*. *Cinema Journal*, **19**(2), 25–40. DOI: https://doi.org/10.2307 /1224869

van Elferen, Isabella (2012). The Gothic Bach. *Understanding Bach*, 7, 9–20.

Verona, Gabriella Gentili (1964). Le collezioni Foà e Giordano della Biblioteca Nazionale di Torino. *Accademie e biblioteche d'Italia* 32, 405–30.

Vincendeau, Ginette (2003). *Jean-Pierre Melville: An American in Paris*. London: British Film Institute. DOI: https://doi.org/10.5040/9781838710156

Waldersee, Paul Graf (1885). Antonio Vivaldis Violinconcerte unter besonderer Berücksichtigung der von Johann Sebastian Bach bearbeiteten. *Vierteljahrsschrift für Musikwissenschaft*, **1**, 356–80.

Wiebe, H. (2012). *Britten's Unquiet Pasts: Sound and Memory in Postwar Reconstruction*. Cambridge: Cambridge University Press. DOI: https://doi .org/10.1017/CBO9780511978951.004

Wierzbicki, James (2009). *Film Music: A History*. New York: Routledge. DOI: https://doi.org/10.4324/9780203884478

Williams, Peter F. (1981). BWV 565: a Toccata in D minor for Organ by J. S. Bach? *Early Music,* **9**(3), 330–7.

Winkler, Max (2010). The Origin of Film Music. In Mervyn Cooke (ed.), *A Hollywood Film Reader.* Oxford: Oxford University Press, pp. 5–13.

Acknowledgements

My thanks to Mervyn Cooke for his guidance, encouragement and friendship. I am very grateful to the two anonymous readers; their comments were immensely useful and I hope my final version reflects that. I would also like to extend my gratitude to Joshua Rifkin, Laura Anderson and Claire Fontijn for reading drafts of the article and offering valuable corrections and suggestions. Thanks also to Laura Anderson for allowing me to see a draft of her article on *Les Enfants terribles*. Last but not least, I thank John Frankish, who was always there with advice, understanding and friendship, and who, halfway down the M2 to Canterbury and faraway in time, first started me thinking about baroque music and cinema.

Cambridge Elements ≡

Music Since 1945

Mervyn Cooke
University of Nottingham

Mervyn Cooke brings to the role of series editor an unusually broad range of expertise, having published widely in the fields of twentieth-century opera, concert and theatre music, jazz, and film music. He has edited and co-edited *Cambridge Companions to Britten, Jazz, Twentieth-Century Opera*, and *Film Music*. His other books include *Britten: War Requiem, Britten and the Far East, A History of Film Music, The Hollywood Film Music Reader, Pat Metheny: The ECM Years*, and two illustrated histories of jazz. He is currently co-editing (with Christopher R. Wilson) *The Oxford Handbook of Shakespeare and Music*.

About the Series

Elements in Music Since 1945 is a highly stimulating collection of authoritative online essays that reflects the latest research into a wide range of musical topics of international significance since the Second World War. Individual Elements are organised into constantly evolving clusters devoted to such topics as art music, jazz, music and image, stage and screen genres, music and media, music and place, immersive music, music and movement, music and politics, music and conflict, and music and society. The latest research questions in theory, criticism, musicology, composition and performance are also given cutting-edge and thought-provoking coverage. The digital-first format allows authors to respond rapidly to new research trends, with contributions being updated to reflect the latest thinking in their fields, and the essays are enhanced by the provision of an exciting range of online resources.

Cambridge Elements ≡

Music Since 1945

Elements in the Series

Music Transforming Conflict
Ariana Phillips-Hutton

Herbert Eimert and the Darmstadt School: The Consolidation of the Avant-Garde
Max Erwin

Baroque Music in Post-War Cinema: Performance Practice and Musical Style
Donald Greig

A full series listing is available at: www.cambridge.org/em45

Printed in the United States
by Baker & Taylor Publisher Services